FORD
FARM TRACTORS
OF THE 1950S

RANDY LEFFINGWELL

MBI Publishing Company

First published in 2001 by MBI Publishing Company,
729 Prospect Avenue, PO Box 1, Osceola, WI 54020-0001 USA

The information in this book is true and complete to the best
of our knowledge. All recommendations are made without any
guarantee on the part of the author or Publisher, who also
disclaim any liability incurred in connection with the use of
this data or specific details.

We recognize that some words, model names and
designations, for example, mentioned herein are the property
of the trademark holder. We use them for identification
purposes only. This is not an official publication.

MBI Publishing Company books are also available at discounts
in bulk quantity for industrial or sales-promotional use.
For details write to Special Sales Manager at Motorbooks
International Wholesalers & Distributors, 729 Prospect
Avenue, Osceola, WI 54020-0001 USA.

Library of Congress Cataloging-in-Publication Data
Leffingwell, Randy.
    Ford farm tractors of the 1950s / Randy Leffingwell.
        p. cm. — (Enthusiast color series)
    Includes index.
    ISBN 0-7603-0908-6 (pbk. : alk. paper)
        1. Ford tractors—History. 2. Farm tractors—United
    States—History. I. Title. II. Series.
    TL233.6.F66 L4423 2001
    631.3'72'0973—dc21   00-048202

On the front cover: **1950 Fordson E27N and 1958 Ford 740**
The vast differences between the 1950 Fordson E27N and the
1958 Ford 740 illustrate the contrast in philosophies between
Ford in England and Ford in the United States. Both tractors
addressed the needs of farmers in their respective countries.

On the frontispiece: **1958 Ford 861**
With the 1958 tractors, Ford sought to make a bolder styling
statement with its coarsely gridded grill. In addition, its
product planners determined that model names would appeal
to buyers, and that year they launched the Workmaster
(134-cid engines) and Powermaster (172-cid engines) series.

On the title page: **1959 Ford 841 Four Wheel Drive**
Each of the Powermaster's 172-cid engine's 50 gross
horsepower was needed to make the best use of the traction
operators got with Ford and Elwood Engineering Company's
four-wheel-drive configuration. Elwood sold the kits to
individuals or through Ford dealers for installation. This
tractor is fitted with a Ford Model 101 three-bottom plow.

On the back cover: **1959 Ford 871
Select-0-Speed Demonstrator**
Production figures vary on these gold promotional tractors.
Some sources now say that Ford offered one model to each of
2,300 Ford dealers in 1959 and the company built that many.
Other figures at Ford indicate that Highland Park
manufactured 861 of them, since many dealerships were too
small to need or afford a demonstrator.

Designed by Bruce Leckie

Edited by Darwin Holmstrom

Printed in China

Contents

Acknowledgments

Ford farm tractors manufactured in the 1950s have so far attracted only a few of the many collectors interested in Ford's agricultural products. In my opinion, these are individuals with vision and foresight and it is they who inspired me to undertake this book.

First and foremost, I'm grateful to the inventors, Harold Brock, Waterloo, Iowa; Eddie Pinardi, Dearborn, Michigan; Ralph Christensen, Badger, South Dakota; Delbert Heusinkveldt, Sioux Center, Iowa; and Joe Funk, Coffeyville, Kansas. In addition, I must thank my colleague, fellow author and historian Stuart Gibbard, for his excellent history of Dagenham and its products. Further, I wish to thank authors (and friends) Guy Fay and Lorry Dunning for their ongoing support and encouragement and for tireless research on my behalf. I owe further thanks to former Ford tractor dealers Don Horner, Geneva, Ohio; and Harold Ypma, Ladysmith, Wisconsin; for their recollections of things past.

For the tractors that appear in this book, I owe deep thanks to Dick, Sheila, and Adam Bosch, Kandyohi, Minnesota; Art and Lillian Bright, LeGrand, California; Roger and Jane Elwood, Lakeville, Conneticut; Dwight and Katie Emstrom, Galesburg, Illinois; Palmer and Harriet Fossum, Northfield, Minnesota; Don Hagstrom, Merino, Colorado; Edith Heidrick and the late Joe Heidrick Collection, Woodland, California; Delbert Heusinkveldt, Iowa; Royal and Karen Hoyer, Miller, Missouri; Ron and Linda Lamoly, New Salem, Massachusetts; William and Treva Lucabough, Glen Rock, Pennsylvania; Paul and Dorothy Martin, Marion, Iowa; Doug Norman, his brother Dale and his son Jim, Montevideo, Minnesota; Rufus and Dorothy Roberts, Cortland, Ohio; and Carlton Sather, Northfield, Minnesota.

To all of you who opened your memories or your barns, pumped up tires and washed tractors, recalled names and dates and events, or who introduced me to others who did, I give my most sincere thanks and hope that you enjoy this brief Ford history.
—Randy Leffingwell
Ojai, California

Introduction

Fordson tractors taught the manufacturing world a few lessons. Nearly 100 companies competed with Henry Ford from the 1910s through the 1920s for a share of the tractor market. Those that survived Ford's relentless competition did their homework well. Ford proved that automotive-type engines, those small displacement power plants operating at higher speeds, could hold up to agriculture's challenges. He also made it clear that producing masses of the same tractor on an assembly line offered economies so great that he made a profit even as he cut prices.

The Fordson came first. Stone simple and far from perfect, it still became England's official wartime tool for food production. But, though Henry was an inveterate tinkerer, he was a reluctant innovator. He held on to ideas and products long after others had found flaws and made improvements in similar machines. Even after he ended production of the Model F Fordson in the United States in 1928, he continued building it in England as the Model N—still strong, still unsophisticated, and still imperfect. After Henry started Fordson production in Cork, Ireland, in 1929 and expanded it into Dagenham, England, in late 1931, he set out to develop the Fordson's replacement.

1963 Ford 2000 The earliest 2000s used the 661's four-cylinder gas engine, the Red Tiger 172-cid powerplant. At Nebraska, this developed 30.5 drawbar horsepower at 2,000 rpm. By 1965 the 2000 would use the Super Dexta's three-cylinder engine and offer just 26.4 horsepower but at nearly a 20 percent improvement in fuel economy.

Ford's experimental efforts for the U. S. replacement were scattershot, just as they had been leading up to the Fordson. His engineers investigated and attempted all manners of ideas. Ford's target became clear when Irish inventor and promoter Harry Ferguson showed up. Ferguson's tractor, sophisticated but still imperfect, evolved into Ford's 9N, another mass-produced, bargain-priced machine. This one, however, introduced the three-point hitch and provided reliable draft control with dedicated implements.

Ferguson had annoyed Ford management and engineers in England who, instead of adopting his idea, slightly revised their steady Fordson Model N. As the prospects of a second war in Europe intensified, Dagenham's management chose to postpone introducing anything new, especially something that might force farmers to replace existing implements in a wartime economy. As it turned out, both Ford in England and in the United States chose correctly for their farmers, but these decisions split Ford's tractor philosophy. By the end of the war, their paths were set. Into the late 1940s and through the 1950s, the period covered in this book, Ford Motor Company operated as two competing tractor manufacturers. Through the 1950s and into the 1960s, it took extraordinary peacekeeping efforts to hold it all together.

1

1946–1952

The Major, the 8N, and History

Ford Motor Company in Dearborn, Michigan, and its British counterpart at Dagenham, England, wasted no time returning to full tractor production after the end of World War II. While both companies carried over existing models, they had begun to conceive and design improved and upgraded versions. Dagenham was ready before Dearborn and on March 19, 1945, its first Fordson E27N rolled off the production line. Ford told the agricultural press that it had named the tractor the Major to make clear to farmers that this model was new and that it offered significant engineering improvements over the previous blue-body, orange-wheel Fordson Model N.

1951 Ford 8N

At its peak, Ford's 8N constituted 25 percent of new tractor sales. A product of Harry Ferguson's collaboration with Henry Ford, the 8N incorporated many improvements both Ford and Ferguson felt were necessary.

The majority of industry in England continued to work under the direction of various boards, committees, and organizations created to manage resources and to get the best out of the work force that was still at home. The War Agricultural Committee still dictated tractor and implement specifications, and it was this body that told Dagenham to provide three-plow capability for its new machine, offer greater ground clearance, and incorporate a center-positioned power takeoff (PTO). While the N-series engine was up to the work of pulling the additional plow, the design engineers created a new rear axle using bull gears and a spiral bevel drive,

because the decades-old Dearborn-designed worm drive would never accommodate the new load. In addition, engineers achieved more ground clearance as a byproduct of the new rear-end design. To bring the nose up and level the tractor, they then revised the front axle by inverting the king pins downward to the wheel hubs.

The row-crop Major provided buyers with steering brakes and adjustable front and rear treads. The most significant options that Dagenham offered were two different hydraulic three-point lift-hitch systems. One was manufactured by Smiths, which farmers operated by a single control lever; the other, by

1947 2N and 1947 8N   The 2N, left, is serial number 305295, and its engine block was cast June 6, 1947. The 8N on the right is serial number 637, and its engine was cast the same day. Internally, the 8N carried a fourth gear but otherwise most changes were visible: paint, air intake, grille badges, and front and rear wheel hubs were improved.

1948 8N   The designation "8N" represented introductory model year, 1948, and the N was Ford's internal code for tractors. The 8N brought the flip-down grille, from engineer Harold Brock's idea and stylist Clare Kramer's design for easier cleaning. The 8Ns also introduced recirculating ball steering systems, slightly higher steering wheels, flip-up seats, and running boards.

Varley, used two levers to operate. Both makers drove their hydraulic pumps from the top of the tractor gearbox to avoid infringing on Harry Ferguson's draft control patents. Dagenham offered pneumatic tires in 1946 after several years during which all its models were available only on war-time rationed steel. In addition, the Major introduced optional 12-volt electric starting and electric lights, an improvement over the Fordson N's optional 6-volt system.

With no funds, time, or material resources available to design a new engine, the Major continued on with the 267-cid power plant from the Fordson N, with its simple splash oil lubrication. Engineering did add a water pump. But this was a tired old engine, in production now for nearly 28 years. In 1948, Dagenham introduced models with the Perkins six-cylinder P6TA diesel. This engine developed nearly 45 horsepower at its recommended 1,500 rpm engine speed. Both gas and diesel models continued with the Model N's three-speed forward transmission. Dagenham produced a standard tread ag model, a row-crop version with adjustable-width front axles and adjustable track rear wheels, an industrial version (on solid rubber), and a land-utility model with pneumatic rubber tires. Between 1945 and the introduction of its replacement in 1952, Dagenham manufactured nearly 236,000 Fordson Majors.

In Dearborn, Ford soldiered on with its 2N, known in Dagenham as the "Grey Menace" because it actually competed with the blue Fordson for sales

1948 8N It took farmers no time to want more power from the new 8N. Iowa farmer Delbert Heusinkveld watched South Dakotan Quinton Nilson win the National Plow Terrace Contest in a V-8–powered 9N. Heusinkveld got help from his brothers. They produced their own with a flip-up hood for easier servicing. Heusinkveld eventually sold his idea to the Funk Brothers in Kansas.

in England and Europe. However, plans advanced in Michigan for the 2N's replacement. This new model was first designated a 7N, but when a 1947 introduction proved unreachable, the much-improved Ford became the 8N for 1948. Part of the impetus for the changes and part of the cause of the delay

was the growing disagreement between Henry Ford and Harry Ferguson over tractor design and marketing decisions.

Henry's only son, Edsel, had died in May 1943 and Henry returned from retirement to run Ford Motor Company (FMC). He was 80 and he had suffered a stroke six years earlier. Henry had trusted and relied on Harry Bennett, his former chauffeur, who had elevated himself into company management. Bennett made some business mistakes and caused some hard feelings. Ford's long-time production manager, Charles Sorensen, who was also Henry's friend and devil's advocate, was among many talented and important allies who left FMC during Bennett's reign. (Bennett had engineering chief Laurence Sheldrick and design director Eugene Gregoire fired because they disagreed with him.) But Ford Motor's true financial power rested in two women, Henry's wife, Clara, and Edsel's widow, Eleanor. Together they controlled 45 percent of company stock. Distressed by Bennett's antics and frustrated by Henry's unwillingness to rein in his former driver, they threatened to sell their stock to the public if Henry didn't yield management of the company to

1949 8N High Crop An extra 4 inches of ground clearance helped farmers raising sugarcane in Florida and South Georgia. All of the high-clearance N-series tractors were produced by aftermarket suppliers. But the humid salt air rusted machines badly. Most high-crop collectors know they're in for a total restoration.

his grandson, Edsel's son, Henry II. Henry Ford II obtained an early release from his wartime Naval training in North Chicago, Illinois, and took over the company in September 1945. After examining the books, Henry II (referred to in later years as The Deuce) concluded that tractor operations were too costly and that the agreement with Harry Ferguson had left FMC at a disadvantage. He decided to end his grandfather's handshake agreement with Ferguson in late November 1946. Three months later, Ferguson filed a $251 million lawsuit against Ford for breach of contract and patent infringement. Three months after that, Henry Ford died at age 83.

To further distinguish the post-Ferguson agreement tractors, Henry II created Dearborn Motors Company (DMC) in November 1946. This was the marketing, sales, and service arm of FMC to handle farm tractors and implements that FMC manufactured. This also allowed Henry II to offer stock options as an inducement to hire top engineering, marketing, and product-planning talent without sacrificing family control of FMC.

Ford's new 8N tractor would be DMC's first product. Harold Brock, the engineer in charge of the new machine, sponsored a vote among engineers and marketing staff for new colors to brighten up the new

1950 Fordson E27N English nomenclature differed from Dearborn's codes. This model's designation was for a 27-horsepower tractor (N) built in England. Dearborn's tractor engineer, Harold Brock, devised the hydraulic system for this model and he got rid of the original worm gear final drive, substituting a bevel final gear.

1950 Fordson E27N In late 1943, Patrick Hennessey started Dagenham's engineers updating the original Fordson F Ministry of Munitions official tractor. Features of the 9N and 2N were attractive, but he feared the costs that would face English farmers when they converted implements to Ferguson's three-point hitch system. Hennessey retained the drawbar. Dagenham offered steel wheels after Dearborn discontinued them.

product. But because he gathered and counted the votes, he adopted the colors of a favorite dress of his wife's, one that was red and silver-gray.

The first production 8N tractor appeared in late 1947. (In 1948, Dagenham produced more than 50,000 Majors. It had turned out more than 150,000 copies of the Fordson N, compared to Dearborn's nearly 200,000 Model 2N tractors.) The 8N added a fourth speed to the gearbox, and Harold Brock's engineers relocated both brake pedals to the right side, making it much easier to slow or stop the tractor smoothly.

With these two models set, Dagenham's Fordson Major and DMC's Ford 8N, FMC entered the 1950s, a period of optimism and growth in population, financial wealth, and technical advances.

American President Harry Truman appointed General George Marshall as U.S. Secretary of State. The general launched the European Recovery Plan, commonly called the Marshall Plan, to aid in the repair, restoration, and re-creation of the European economy. U.S. voters re-elected Truman to a second term, while in England, Prime Minister Clement Attlee ended bread rationing and nationalized the railroads. As the new decade began, the United States recorded a population of 150,700,000 while the world held nearly 2.3 billion. Clement Attlee recognized Communist China, North Korea invaded the south, and Harry Truman instructed the Atomic Energy Commission to develop a hydrogen bomb.

Through 1951 and 1952, Harry Ferguson's lawsuit against FMC slogged on in and out of the courtroom. Prior to the March 29, 1951, opening arguments, nearly 200 lawyers and many more aides on both sides had gathered nearly 1 million pages of evidence. Harry Ferguson's deposition alone ran 10,312 pages.

As the economy in Europe began its gradual recovery, gasoline prices, which historically had been high in Europe, crept up even more. Farmers could afford distillate fuel, but it offered lower performance per gallon. Dagenham had hoped for a favorable response to its Perkins diesel engine program, and it was pleased when sales figures indicated the E27N

1951 Ford 8N   This is a treasure that collectors dream about. This tractor had only 123.8 hours on it when these photos were shot. Illinois Ford collector Dwight Emstrom knew about this machine for some time. His persistence paid off. With original tires, rubber hoses, and belts, this will remain unrestored, as a "time capsule" and also as indication of how Ford really assembled its tractors.

1951 Ford 8N High Crop   Outside specialists began producing high-clearance equipment for Southern farmers toward the end of 9N production. Their products became more numerous in 2N configurations. When Ford introduced its 8N, the aftermarket makers had their tools and dies in place. For them the biggest difference was paint color.

Major was England's most popular diesel-powered tractor. The company sold nearly 23,000 of them between 1948 and the end of production in 1952. Diesel power had been a leap of faith on the part of Dagenham's general manager, Patrick Hennessey. Hennessey was a principal participant in the efforts to have Britain's Ministry of Munitions adopt Ford's Fordson as its official tractor in 1917, and he had been promoted through several titles by 1944. At that time, he approved a development program for Dagenham's own diesel. His engineers completed the project and Dagenham introduced it at the agriculture show at Smithfield in London in November 1951, as the New Fordson Major. Regular production of this tractor, known internally as the E1A, made models available to buyers in early 1952.

Recognizing that designing and casting the engine block is a major portion of the development and production expense, Hennessey's engineers used the basic new 3.6-liter block for tractor vaporizing oil (TVO) gasoline and diesel fuels, varying the compression ratio from a low of 4.25:1 for TVO, and 5.5:1 for gasoline, up to 16:1 for diesel. Both TVO and gas engines were designed with 3.74-inch bore and 4.52-inch stroke for 199 cid. The diesel got larger bore, at 3.94 inches, but the same stroke, resulting in 220-ci displacement. All three engines developed 35 horsepower at 1,600 rpm. Simplifying engine production in this way delivered a volume manufacturing economy to Ford, allowing Dagenham to keep the diesel's costs well below competitors. (Another advantage was that Dagenham's engineers had developed an easy-starting diesel; TVO

1952 Ford 8N with Dearborn Harvester Dearborn Motors opened its doors in January 1947, marketing tractors that FMC produced in the United States, and distributing implements built by outside manufacturers. Wood Brothers of Des Moines, Iowa, provided Dearborn Motors with a full line of crop picking and harvesting equipment.

still required operators to start it on gasoline and switch over to the vaporizing oil once the engine had reached operating temperature. This cumbersome system was still temperamental, even after all these years. The diesel quickly eclipsed TVO sales as word spread of its economy of operation and ease of starting. TVO engines completely disappeared in 1957.)

Dagenham's engineers now offered 12-volt electrics as standard equipment along with a hydraulic three-point hitch. They modified and improved the transmission, still providing only three gears but now in two ranges. Dagenham produced standard utility tractor models mostly, but it also turned out a few row-crop tricycles and some high-clearance models.

In the United States, DMC's 8N was never a "Red-and-silver-gray menace" to Dagenham's sales fleet because Dearborn chose not to export it. DMC was selling all it could produce in the United States anyway. DMC introduced the 8N at $1,000 in 1948. In 1950, Engineering relocated the distributor to the side of the engine from its previously nearly inaccessible position underneath the water pump. Over its life, the tractor's weight had increased from 2,410 pounds to 2,490 pounds, some of the gain attributable to a change in 1949 from a worm-and-sector steering system carried over from the 2N models to a ball-screw-type system. In addition, Dearborn fitted running boards and a tip-up seat, so farmers could operate the tractor while standing. Ford also offered a

1952 Ford 8N with Dearborn 1-way Plow   This 18-inch plow provided an automatic reset feature. Pulling a single lever raised one bottom at the end of the row. Pulling the same lever again dropped the opposite plow at the start of the next. Releasing both levers dropped both plows and enabled farmers to use the implement as a trencher/ditcher as well.

1952 Ford 8N with Dearborn Road Maintainer Dearborn's catalog was extensive and included this Meili-Blumberg Model 19-35 road grader for mounting on Ford's 8N or 2N models. M-B was located in New Holstein, Wisconsin. The Model 19-35 stretched out the small tractor, yielding a 14-foot wheelbase and a 39-foot turn circle. Combined weight was 6,900 pounds.

distillate fuel version, the 8NAN, now exceedingly rare and desirable to collectors, that produced just 23 horsepower from its lower 4.75:1 compression. Overall, however, Ford's 8N sold as well as most Ford tractor models had done before, about 400,000 copies through 1952. But the handwriting was on the wall; the days of the Ford-Ferguson-derived machines were numbered. And the number was small.

On April 9, 1952, Harry Ferguson accepted U.S. Judge Gregory Noonan's settlement agreement with Ford. Dearborn Motors reimbursed Ferguson $9.25 million for patent infringements only, and no penalties, nothing like the $251 million figure Ferguson had sought. During the 54 weeks of the trial, many of Ferguson's patents had entered the public domain. Ford agreed to discontinue production of the hydraulic system using Ferguson's reservoir-side

hydraulic fluid pump by the end of the 1952 model year. In so many words, it meant DMC had to take the 8N out of production at the end of that year. Ferguson, who had begun producing Ford 9N look-alikes that he marketed as Ferguson TE-20 and TO-20 (for Tractor, Europe, 20 horsepower, and Tractor, Overseas, 20 horsepower), suffered in the final settlement for his success. He had manufactured nearly 140,000 of the 9N clones without Ford's permission for the tractor design.

Dearborn Motors already had a successor waiting. It was Henry II's idea, a tribute to his grandfather and his devotion to farm tractors, in honor of the corporation's fiftieth anniversary. DMC's product-planning groups, always happy to have something new to plan, produce, and promote, liked the idea and they pushed for the Golden Jubilee model.

1952 Ford 8N-C pump   Yet another Dearborn Motors product, the Model C pump, mated the 8N engine to a variety of pump heads, all provided by Funk Brothers (of engine conversion kit fame.) Another variation on this, though even rarer than the pump, was the power unit, fitting the 8N to a 6,000-watt generator set for farm power.

1952 Ford 8N Half-Track
Still another Dearborn option was this Blackhawk Half-Track, produced by the ARPS Corporation, also from New Holstein, Wisconsin. This Model BM, #2141, fit 8N or 2N models. ARPS produced about 14,000 of these kits to convert tractors to heavy snow or sand use and made systems for Ford and other manufacturers as well.

2

1953–1954

Fiftieth Anniversary Jubilee and other Powerful Ideas

Back in 1943, Harold Brock and fellow engineer Dale Roeder had worked on a large tractor project in Dearborn dubbed the 4P for four-plow tractor. This was a kind of steroid-swollen 2N that provided about 45 percent more power in a tractor some 40 percent heavier than the 2N. This development program was driven by a competitive urge to offer a larger machine that would put Ford on farms currently running International Harvester W-9, Case LA, and Minneapolis-Moline GTA tractors. Brock and Roeder designed the 4P using many parts taken directly from 2N production. However, after five prototypes and

1953 Ford NAA Golden Jubilee   The Golden Jubilee was Henry Ford II's homage to his grandfather, Henry Ford. Engineering stretched the 8N wheelbase 4 inches for better stability, also making possible cultivators mounted below the tractor. Eddie Pinardi's wheat medallion, designed by Ford's Styling Department, became the tractor logo for a decade.

23

1953 Ford NAA Golden Jubilee   Production of the Ford Golden Jubilee began in September 1952. The first of the 1953s reached dealers before Thanksgiving. This was Ford's first new tractor since the Harry Ferguson–inspired 9N. Ford fitted the "Red Tiger" I-block four-cylinder overhead-valve engine, and added a new independent hydraulic pump and PTO, quite different from Ferguson's system.

nearly $1 million spent on design, construction, and testing, both Edsel and Henry Ford withdrew support and the project died. But its legacy was a few lasting lessons that reappeared with the Golden Jubilee when it was publicly introduced on January 3, 1953.

Brock and Roeder again met to work on this new model, designated the NAA. Work began in 1951 with designers and engineers still within FMC. The 163 staff engineers working at DMC had other obligations: designing, developing, and testing implements. The NAA was to be Ford's first new tractor since Harry Ferguson, and Brock and Roeder's work on the 4P had provided them with some valuable information. They stretched the 8N wheelbase and overall length by 4 inches, giving it more stability and weight up front. They created a new inline four-cylinder engine they called the Red Tiger. This engine had overhead valves, making it taller, and engineers repositioned the muffler alongside the top of the engine. This increased the height of the tractor 4 inches as well.

1954 Ford NAA   The Golden Jubilee model was a one-year designation honoring the 50th anniversary, a fact that Ford celebrated only with its tractor models. There was no automobile or truck counterpart. As Ferguson hitch patents began to expire, Ford and others adopted the designs.

1951 Ford 8N with V-8 C-60 The quest for power led Quinton Nilson to adopt Ford's flathead truck V-8, a combination that Delbert Heusinkveld stuck with as well. Both men had to extensively modify the tractor's hood and appearance. Connecticut collector/restorer Roger Elwood wondered if it were possible to install a V-8 without interrupting the original hood line.

A host of improvements included a heavily revised hydraulic system with a new vane-type hydraulic pump and "Hy-trol" flow control and its own fluid reservoir. Engineering replaced the vane pump with a piston pump during 1953 production. Brock and Roeder made live PTO an option, operated by the hydraulic clutch with its own pump. Among standard equipment specifications, Brock's group replaced the governor and the rear-axle brakes and seals. The group completely revised the hydraulics, partially to satisfy the Ferguson settlement but equally to take advantage of ongoing development improvements it had made. Buyers could add optional remote hydraulic cylinders for front-mounted implements. Various improvements, upgrades on equipment and

parts, new standard equipment, and the tractor's slightly enlarged size added barely 100 pounds to the weight of the NAA over the previous Model 8N. Ford's Styling Department designed handsome sheet metal that was a smart evolution from styling chief Eugene Gregoire's "streamline era" 9N into a kind of "industrial machine" look that came to characterize farm tractors of the 1950s. Manufacture started in Dearborn in September 1952, and the earliest production models were delivered to waiting customers before Thanksgiving. It was named the "Golden Jubilee," both words connoting 50 years of time passage.

"I was involved in the development and testing of the NAA," Eddie Pinardi recalled. Pinardi and his brother, Charles, worked for Harold Brock in Tractor Engineering for more than 20 years. Eddie began in 1937 as a draftsman, as everyone in Ford engineering did in those days. When he retired 50 years later, his was the final signature everyone needed to sign off engineering drawings before they went into production.

"That NAA went all right," Pinardi said. "In fact, I was the one who made the Jubilee nameplate. I didn't do it alone. I was the one who made the drawing for that, with the gold and the wheat, the wheat medallion." While it sounds simple enough to do, it was laced with politics.

"That was a heck of a thing to come up with," Pinardi continued. "In those days, you made a design and then you sent it down to Dearborn, down to the stylists. They'd do their idea and it would come back and you'd send it back down and say, 'Give it to me this way.'

"The stylists thought the wheats were too narrow. Should have been wider. The proportion wasn't right. The wheat stalks came down too fast to a point; it should have come down slower and been wider at the bottom. The word 'Ford' wasn't made right, the letters weren't right. Oh, gosh, just everything. They had comments and ideas and suggestions about everything.

"If Styling at Dearborn said it was not right, there wasn't much you could do about it. But finally, it *was* right. We agreed to it."

In the early 1950s, FMC still sold tractors only to regional distributors who supplied their dealers. Regions might cover an entire state or, in the agricultural Midwest, just a portion of one. It was a system developed during the earliest Fordson tractor and Model T automobile days.

Don Horner was a Ford tractor dealer in Geneva, Ohio, who inherited Horner Implement Co. from his father, who had started in the late 1920s producing golf-course tractors based on shortened Model T

chassis. He built 17 before an opportunity came along to sell Irish Fordsons and later the Dagenham-built machines. Tractors came from a distributor in Columbus. When Ford and Ferguson split in 1947, Horner's supplier left Ford and followed Ferguson. An Oklahoma distributor, Tom Hayward, acquired the Columbus operation and at that point, Don Horner began to sell 8Ns and Dearborn Motors implements. He got word from Hayward in the fall of 1952 that Ford had a new tractor and Hayward invited him for a show.

"In late October 1952, we went to Columbus to the Ohio Theater for the introduction of the Jubilee," Horner said. "It was a real show. Then they rolled out the tractor. After it came on the stage and we got to admire it from a distance, they took us by bus back to Tom Hayward's distributorship to touch the metal.

"Now this was a tractor that a lot of people were waiting for. This was an area [northeast Ohio] and a time where there were a lot of 50-, 60-acre farms and people were making a good living off these small farms. For these people, the Jubilee tractor was the next step up from the 9N they had had for 10 years now or for the 8N they just bought a year before.

"The Jubilee engine was called the Red Tiger, but it was really nothing but a four-cylinder version of the I-block six, the first overhead-valve six-cylinder that Ford made for civilian use.

"Right after our introduction at Columbus, we got our first Jubilees, right away," Horner said. "And we had an open house at our dealership. Coffee and sandwiches. No hard liquor like they had for the dealers at Columbus, just pop. And, boy, the people came. They came from all over. And they bought 'em, right off the floor." Horner recognized the work that went into the new tractors, and he admired the appearance. He knew it helped sell the tractors. So did its name.

"The Jubilee was the 1953," Eddie Pinardi explained. "The one with the wheat medallion.

1951 Ford 8N with V-8 C-60 . Converting an 8N to V-8 power was not an easy task but one requiring thousands of hours to fabricate engine mounts, frame rails (as Funk had to do with its early six-cylinder kits) and other pieces. Roger Elwood revised the factory exhaust system to fit the tractor complete with its mufflers. The installation required extensive modification to equipment beneath the sheet metal.

That was the NAA. The NBA was 1954. But you can't really say that. The NAA in 1953 wasn't the same as the NAA in 1955. And the NAA was the work tractor, like a utility, an industrial . . ., but you could have plows put on it. The NBA was the agricultural tractor. There were just too many changes. They just added on, they just changed the letters going up one in the alphabet each year, NAA, NBA, NCA, like that, until they got to the big ones, the Hundreds series."

Pinardi's boss, Harold Brock, remembered the nomenclature. He is sometimes amused by tractor collectors and historians trying to find significance in every detail.

"The letters NAA didn't stand for anything," he said. "They were just the next letters available. The 9N, 2N, and 8N were the years they were brought out. Then they got into planning and . . ."

The product planners at DMC weren't the only ones thinking about changes. In late May 1953, six months after introducing the Jubilee, FMC in Dearborn, satisfied with the business arrangements made possible by the creation of Dearborn Motors, reorganized tractor production and distribution once

1951 Ford 8N flathead 6   Early Funk conversion kits to fit Ford's flathead six required the twin-rail subframe to support the long industrial engine. Joe Funk credited Milford, Illinois, Ford tractor dealer Olaf E. Glover with the idea. Funk saw the modification while selling Glover Funk gears. Glover told Funk to take the idea and run with it.

more. It acquired DMC as a wholly owned subsidiary, under the umbrella of Ford Tractor Division (FTD), which established offices in nearby Birmingham, Michigan. Charged with research, planning, production, marketing, and distribution, the new FTD staff took over where DMC's planners had stopped, contemplating the direction in which future tractor design should go. They had to, because everybody else was looking far ahead as well. By 1953, John Deere's chairman, Charles Deere Wiman, had already concluded that his company's two-cylinder tractors had reached the limit of performance capability. He authorized what became a seven-year-long program to create a new generation of Deere tractors. Similar projects within International Harvester would bring engineering and appearance changes.

Underlying all of this was another parameter, another need, another bragging right. For Ford, IHC, and Deere engineering departments, it offered tough challenges. For marketing and sales, it was another opportunity to get customers into the sales agencies. For accounting departments and shareholders, it represented millions of dollars in development and testing costs. What it meant to the farmer was the ability to do more work in a day. If the first great tractor war had been started by Henry Ford's Fordson pricing against all the competition, this period of time—the mid-point of the century—launched the second great tractor war: the battle for horsepower. But unlike tractor price and sales wars that ended in the furrows, this one began there. For it was often the farmers themselves, inveterate tinkers and inventors, that kept looking at their own machines and asking "what if?"

Henry Ford probably would have appreciated Quinton Nilson. Any time Ford got his hands on a new machine or invention, he worked at improving it. Nilson, farming near Spink, South Dakota, did the same thing with a 9N tractor. He felt it needed more power, which led him to install a Ford flathead V-8. When it came time on Tuesday morning, September 20, 1949, for the National Plow Terrace Contest at West Point, Nebraska, every manufacturer was there with new tractors and expert operators. But Quinton believed he had a chance to show them all real performance.

The Nilson farm near the Big Sioux River had needed terracing to control soil erosion, and Quinton became good at carving up and leveling off the land. He and his father had just completed a 12-year conservation program on their 250-acre farm, creating 10 miles of terraces and two big dams. To work faster, he replaced the 9N engine with the Mercury V-8 95. At the contest, before 12,000 spectators, he won hands down.

"He wasn't plowing," Delbert Heusinkveld recalled, "he was throwing dirt." Heusinkveld is another person Henry Ford might have appreciated. But he didn't start tinkering until he'd seen Quinton Nilson. "It took him just 20 minutes to do the job. The second place took an hour."

Wednesday's Omaha *World-Herald* commented: "Mr. Nilson's souped-up machine isn't just a freak he devised to win the contest. He uses it on his farm. It pulls a two-bottom plow at 13 miles an hour, considerably better than a conventional tractor. The more powerful motor and double set of rear wheels were his own ideas.

"Maybe souped-up engines and jet propulsion won't power the tractor of the future," the newspaper wrote. "But who knows? Ingenious fellows like Mr. Nilson start other people thinking about [doing] things faster and better. Then anything can happen."

Delbert Heusinkveld and his brothers were among those 12,000 spectators watching Nilson throw dirt. They farmed in Springfield, Nebraska, with their dad and his 9N. They also felt it lacked power. Delbert and his brothers Marion, Glenn, and Garrett had each studied the V-8 engine in the family's 1935 Ford. Delbert even measured it. It was 2 inches too long. But when the 1948 pickup trucks appeared with removable bellhousings and side-mounted distributors, Delbert figured that might work without needing to change the tractor frame.

Heusinkveld located a shop in Sioux City, Iowa, to fabricate an adapter. While that was being made, the brothers went to the contest, watched Quinton, and later got to know him. When Delbert went back to pick up his adapter, the shop owner mentioned Funk Aircraft in Coffeyville, Kansas. Funk had just begun to produce kits to install Ford industrial six-cylinder engines in the N-series tractors.

Delbert and his brothers finished their conversion with help from cousins who did body-work,

1952 Ford 8N with overhead-valve six   Later Funk conversion kits used Ford's industrial overhead-valve six-cylinder engines. Joe and Howard Funk adapted Delbert Heusinkveld's idea of using a cast-iron oil pan to support the engine, replacing the side rails. This allowed both Funk ohv-6 and V-8 engines' conversions to function as unit-frames.

splitting the hood to accommodate the wider engine, and widening the grille by two inches.

"I had to widen the hood," Heusinkveld explained, "to fit in a bigger radiator and the six-bladed truck fan. The minute we went that route, cooling became a dream. Before, the temperature gauge just kept creeping up." Delbert exchanged other ideas with Quinton, and when Heusinkveld's second V-8 was done, he and Nilson together

hauled it down to Coffeyville to show Joe and Howard Funk.

Howard and Joe Funk had worked with Ford for decades, beginning with adapting extensively modified four-cylinder Model B water-cooled engines to their own aircraft in Akron, Ohio. After building 110 aircraft, the Funks went broke. They moved to Coffeyville, working with a pump maker who loved their airplanes. Immediately after World War II, Joe and

1952 Ford 8N with flathead V-8   So far as collectors see things now, Joe and Howard Funk's finest hour was the period in which they made kits to fit Ford's flathead V-8s into Ford's N-series tractors. Initially, the Funks designed the kit so that factory manifolds dumped the exhaust into pipes running below the tractor. But inverted manifolds let short pipes run straight up, adding noise appeal to the rare models. Funk produced only 225 kits for V-8s.

Howard returned to airplanes, building 350 before bankruptcy stopped them again.

The machine shop they'd developed to fabricate their planes became their salvation and they quit aircraft for earthbound machines. They began producing Harold Brock's transmissions for Ford tractors in the early 1950s. Their catalog contained hundreds of gears, adapters, mounting systems, and converters. One day in 1950 they called on Olaf Glover, the Ford tractor dealer in tiny Milford, Illinois. Glover showed them a 9N tractor which he had just fitted with Ford's industrial inline six-cylinder engine. Glover, a repairman and mechanic, not a machinist, had crudely welded an adapter and side-support frame rails from the radiator to the transmission housing to support the longer, heavier engine. This framework provided a bearing on the front to attach the front axle. Ollie Glover's invention was rough but it provided 100 smooth horsepower to farmers. Joe Funk loved it.

"He had done it with welding," Joe Funk recalled. "Glover was the first spark. Did it first.

Gosh, we came back down here and made fancy patterns and castings, machined it up and worked all the details out and had tremendous instruction books. It was all dealt through Ford tractor dealers.

"We made some six-cylinder conversions for that old boy, Glover. By the time we were done, we made more than five thousand. Got into a few incidents with them, too."

A night shift foreman on Ford's tractor assembly had misunderstood the need for heat treating pinion and ring gears in tractor differentials. He thought it was a cosmetic effect like polishing, so he eliminated the step, which led to hundreds of rear-end failures, most commonly in Funk engine-equipped tractors. They threatened to sue Funk until Joe Funk was able to prove it was lack of heat treating. Ford shut down production and sent technicians around the country to replace every gear that was not heat treated.

"And then they fell in love with us," Funk said with a laugh. "See, we sold five *thousand* industrial engines for them. Through dealers! Not through industrial wholesalers at factory price. *Five thousand!*"

But as significant as that number is, it was the much smaller-production V-8 kit that really made Joe and Howard Funk into legends among Ford tractor enthusiasts.

"When they saw it, they just loved it," Heusinkveld picked up the story again. "They wanted to build tractors just like it. But when we got into widening the hood, they debated for a while. They were sensible guys. They decided widening the hood was not something that every farmer or dealer wanted to fool with.

"So they raised the hood about 6 inches, left the gas tank there, and put a long, narrow radiator in, sped the fan up, things like that. I never liked the looks of theirs, but they worked. We never thought about anybody but Funks. They made the six-cylinders. Sixes did everything the V-8 would do. You didn't need a V-8. That was just a crazy thing of us guys. Sixes had as much power. Oh, it was a homelier outfit, longer. But that was a good engine . . ., and later, in '52, Funks used the overhead-valve engine."

The Funks introduced V-8 kits quickly. Heusinkveld remembered getting promotional brochures in the fall of 1950, a few months after they'd visited the brothers. Neither Quinton nor Delbert ever intended to mass produce V-8 tractors. Nilson was a farmer; after winning the 1949 contest he never returned. Heusinkveld was a trucker and, while he ultimately produced seven completed V-8 tractors, it took too much time from his real work.

"Funk sold only kits," Heusinkveld said. "They made cast-iron oil pans. That's how it came about. I tried talking Sioux City Foundry into making one. The old guy who ran it really liked the idea. He thought about it and finally sat me down. 'The only problem,' he said, 'is for the first one, somebody has to come up with about 10 grand. After that, they'll be cheap.' Pattern making cost was unreal.

"Down at Coffeyville, an old pattern maker got interested in the idea. He told me he was going to try it, for the challenge. He got drawings from Ford archives, made a pattern. When he was done, it bolted up nicely. After that, [the] Funks had him make one for the six-cylinder as well and they got rid of those frame rails they had to add at first."

The Heusinkveld-Nilson V-8 kit became a popular item for the Funk brothers. Its big appeal was the dual exhaust pipes sprouting from below the rear axle. It wasn't until years later that younger farmers reversed exhaust manifolds and ran pipes upward. Funk produced about 225 kits. When more powerful tractors were introduced, production slowed. Leftover kits lined the shelves until recent years when fascination with the power and glory—and the barking exhaust sound—of flathead V-8s brought them out of hiding.

Henry Ford would have loved it.

3

1952–1957

The Impact of Dagenham's Fordson E1A New Major

As evidence of the close family relationship that existed between Ford Motor Company, U.S.A., and Ford Motor Company, Ltd., Harold Brock's 4P prototype got a second breath of life in England. After Henry and Edsel Ford vetoed any further development of the project for the U.S. market, one of Brock's five prototypes surfaced in Dagenham in January 1946. Whether Henry had it shipped over or Patrick Hennessey saw it on one of his frequent visits to Dearborn and asked for it is unknown. But Brock had gone to Dagenham in early 1946 to assist the English engineers with development of a new small tractor. He also worked with them

1956 Fordson Major Dagenham's engineers at Rainham designed the row-crop-configured Major for U.S. markets. They collaborated with Roadless Traction, Ltd., at Hounslow, a firm that manufactured crawler versions of English Ford products. With its diesel engine, the tricycle filled a niche that Dearborn Motors had not yet addressed.

1952 Fordson E1A with Davis Front Loader   Current owner Don Hagstrom inherited this working machine from his father, Paul, who bought it new in Wichita, Kansas, in 1952. Paul added the Davis front loader and three-point-hitch rear blade. Massey-Ferguson eventually acquired Davis.

on evaluating the large four-plow machine to replace the E27N Fordson Major.

Hennessey's engineer Mick Ronayne set to work on a prototype that pulled some ideas from the 4P after Brock returned to the United States at the end of 1946. By late fall of 1947, Ronayne and his staff had produced a full-size wooden mock-up of a tractor with the 4P's sliding-gear four-speed transmission. (The value of forming full-size models of wood was another Brock import. He had learned this technique from both styling and engineering departments in Dearborn. Wood models gave them a chance to see how—and if—pieces fit before spending tens of thousands of dollars on a metal prototype.) Ronayne

added live hydraulics using a Plessy pump driven off the clutch and mounted in front of the transmission. They added a rear axle with adjustable track with sliding wheel hubs. Each of these elements first were specified on blueprints and then carved out of wood to fit on the mock-up. During the next year, Hennessey's engineers produced yet another five running prototypes of the 4P tractors. But at Dagenham, as at Dearborn, practical economics torpedoed the project. As Stuart Gibbard reported in his excellent book, *The Ford Tractor Story, Part One, Dearborn to Dagenham, 1917 to 1964,* Ronayne's boss, tractor department manager Harry Power, canceled the tractor after learning that costs of production tooling would be

1953 Fordson E1A Major   Dagenham exported most of its Fordson Majors to the United States, competing directly with Dearborn Motors' Jubilee model. The Major's success was attributable largely to its diesel engine, which was still several years away from Dearborn's product line. Diesel Majors represented 90 percent of Fordson sales in the United States.

too high. With this, the 4P (or prototype 5035 as it was known at Dagenham while Ronayne worked on it) finally died.

Harry Power concluded instead that matching engines designed by Dagenham engineer Laurie Martland to a new six-speed gearbox derived from the E27N's four-speed transmission would be more cost effective for Ford Ltd. and for British farmers. Another engineer, John Foxwell, created the transmission using an extra set of gears that provided an over- and underdrive, either range engaged by a gear lever mounted on the gearbox. Foxwell's design, according to historian Gibbard, allowed Dagenham to retain the belt pulley mounted on the side of the tractor.

Ronayne, Martland, and Foxwell completed a full-scale, metal-bodied prototype in October 1950, and they had a set of preproduction machines ready for photographs in February 1951. Sir Patrick Hennessey, by then knighted for his work in wartime food production, introduced the tractor over a five-day

Next Page: **1953 Fordson E1A Major**   While Ford Motor Company, Ltd., sold its diesel Majors in 100 countries around the world, its largest market (after the United Kingdom) was the United States, where the Major came in at least $300 less than other diesels. Henry Ford II himself authorized the import and distribution as part of post–World War II economic redevelopment.

1956 Fordson Major   Ford introduced the Row Crop at the Smithfield Show in London in late 1954. It was not meant for U.K. buyers. Roadless created the front twin-wheel structure and support pedestal. Within a year, Dagenham also offered an adjustable rear axle as well, rivaling anything any other domestic U.S. manufacturer offered.

"superb, uncomplicated, and economical." This came, in part, from its Simms injector pump with its pneumatic governor and an "excess fuel" button that made cold starting much easier. It developed 40 horsepower and cost the buyer about £500 pounds (roughly $240 U.S. at the time) more than either the gasoline or TVO models.

Dagenham continued the FMC practice of continuously introducing running upgrades. In 1953 engineering replaced the under-tractor exhaust and muffler with a vertical stack and muffler that lifted the fumes over the operator's head. The diesels sold well enough that Dagenham began designating these most powerful models with a large "D" hood badge. Then in August of that year came one of Dagenham's most significant achievements, a result of nothing less than international politics.

One of the tenets of the U.S. Marshall Plan for European economic recovery was a strategy referred to as "Trade Not Aid." Through this system, the Marshall Plan encouraged nations ravaged by World War II to develop marketable products for a growing consumer population in the United States and elsewhere. Henry Ford II echoed the slogan as he

program to the agricultural media, Ford dealers, government officials and a delegation of foreign trade ministers during late November 1951. Dagenham had 20 tractors on display, including a full crawler modified by County Commercial Cars Ltd. and a half-track produced by Roadless Traction.

Laurie Martland's three engines, all derived from the same block, were the centerpiece of Hennessey's introduction. Of these, the most significant was the new diesel model, designated the E1ADDN (the gas model was the E1AD and the TVO model was the E1ADKN). Gibbard characterized the diesel as approved orders for Dagenham's Diesel Major for delivery to farmers in Texas, Louisiana, and throughout the Midwest. By the end of 1953, Dagenham had shipped $3 million worth of Diesel Majors to DMC for distribution. The Major filled a gaping hole in Dearborn Motors' product lineup—it was the company's only diesel-engine tractor. Because of favorable arrangements between Dearborn and Dagenham, DMC was able to sell the Diesel Majors for $300 to $500 less than the competition such as Deere's new Model R, IHC's WD-40 and Farmall MD, and others. DMC advertised the English Fordson as "The Diesel that Gives You More for Your Money." The United States became Dagenham's largest overseas market and for 1954, Dagenham enhanced its appeal to U.S. farmers when it introduced a tricycle row-crop diesel only for American markets. Roadless Traction produced the modification, delivering its first tractors in August 1953. Roadless offered an adjustable rear axle in September.

As FMC in Dearborn had done with the creation of DMC, so Dagenham operations did in 1955, reorganizing tractor manufacture, sales, design, and planning into a new division. John Foxwell, who had devised the six-speed transmission, was named executive engineer for the new tractor division. Shortly before this, the 500,000th Fordson drove off the Dagenham assembly line. In late June 1955, the assembly line at Rainham Works completed its 100,000th Major.

Foxwell was aware of the New Major's shortcomings, particularly its lack of live PTO and live hydraulics, something available on Dearborn's NAA model now for three years. Dagenham introduced this feature in late 1956, accomplishing the engineering by using two separate friction clutches, each controlling its own driveshaft. Two more

American requests, power steering and a comfort seat, also appeared at the Smithfield agricultural equipment show in London. By the time these updated models first arrived on American farms in May 1957, FMC boasted it had produced 2.5 million tractors in its 40 years; 200,000 of those were diesel New Majors. Dearborn exported very few of the 8N and NAA models. English farmers knew about the technical improvements offered in the new American Fords from reading farming journals, but, since DMC was selling all it could produce, English farmers could not get them. Conversely, DMC imported thousands of Diesel New Majors under terms of the Trade Not Aid program. But more than a few American Ford customers wondered why, if both tractors were built by "Ford," no one seemed to have figured out how to build a row-crop NAA diesel with live PTO and hydraulics. Product planners heard this often. DMC would be ready for 1955 with a new series giving Americans everything, which then forced English farmers to wonder about what *they* were missing.

Foxwell had responded to English farmers' demands for these American features with the Mark II Major, introduced a month earlier in April 1957. Laurie Martland revised his diesel engine, modifying the injectors, cylinder head, camshaft, and rocker arms. Dagenham quoted 51.8 horsepower from the new version. Dagenham's new Tractor Division dropped the TVO engined-model but kept the gasoline version available as an option. Dagenham, all of the United Kingdom and Europe, and now Dearborn, were infected with diesel-mania. Ironically, however, while Dearborn was enlarging its tractors and broadening its line, Dagenham was heading smaller, getting ready to introduce its own version of Dearborn's NAA.

4

1955–1957

Product Planners Inaugurate the Hundred Series

"When Dearborn Motors got organized," Harold Brock explained, "they brought in outside guys from our competition. 'We need to have a product planning group,' they told us. We'd done pretty well with our small group: 25 percent of the business. 'We need to make a tricycle tractor,' they said. 'Like IH, or Case. If we did that, we'd get more market.'

"They persevered. I said, 'Show me the advantages of these tricycle tractors.' They'd get out their cultivators and by the time they found all the parts to bolt on the front and the rear, we'd have been in the field and out.

"'What's the advantage,' I asked them, 'if you're still looking for the parts to bolt on?'

1957 Ford 661   For $2,265, the buyer got optional power steering on this top-of-the-line 600-series model. With live PTO and live hydraulics, this model weighed 3,095 pounds. Its Red Tiger 134-cid engine produced 32.3 gross horsepower.

"The advantage was that we'd be more like all our competitors and that would make all of *them* more comfortable. What they really did was changed something fundamental. Instead of shipping fourteen tractors, all the same, in a boxcar, now you ship them on trucks or flat cars. It cost us more. It confused dealers with more products, spare parts, and replacement pieces. You had the classic design and then . . ."

Even before Ford introduced the Golden Jubilee in late 1952, Harold Brock's tractor engineering group began developing and testing a wide range of new machines. Ford in the United States now would offer tricycle tractors.

"The evolution from the NAA series to the Hundreds . . . ohhh boy," Eddie Pinardi said with a whistle. "From the earliest, with the little Ford-Ferguson, we had a tractor that would pull two plows. Then came the NAA and we had a tractor that could pull three plows.

"Then they wanted a tractor to pull five plows. So we increased everything to pull five plows. Three or four years later, they wanted a tractor that could pull six plows. Everything again had to be increased.

"We knew one thing. We had a tractor that could pull three plows and they wanted one that would pull six. We couldn't just double everything and figure it

1955 Ford Norman Tandem 950-960   With politicians and world leaders, the rule is: Power corrupts, and absolute power corrupts absolutely. In farming, the need for power creates, and the need for more power brings more creativity. Tandem tractors were a quick and easy (though not cheap) solution to the need to get more work done. Simply take two and make one.

1955 Ford Norman Tandem 950-960   By the mid-1950s, Ford, IHC, and other manufacturers offered kits to join two tractors together in tandem. Sometimes tinkerers, inventors, and farmers like Doug Norman saw what was there and liked their own ideas better. With 344 ci and nearly 100 horsepower between the two tricycles, Norman pulled five bottoms.

would work. The more we pulled, the bigger we had to make it. And there was the model year change. Like cars, they wanted a new tractor every fall."

Mechanized farming was changing. In 1917 there were just 15,525 tractors on farms in the United States. Production in 1918, the first year the Fordson was widely available, was an impressive 132,697, of which 96,470 sold. By the end of 1920, farmers in the United States were using 246,083 tractors.

That number doubled in 1925 to 505,933 tractors as farmers recovered from the economic hardships of the post–World War I early 1920s and

became more cognizant of the benefits of power farming. In 1930 the U.S. Department of Agriculture (USDA) attributed a 30 percent increase in crop yield over yields five years earlier to better designed, more efficient, more affordable tractors and implements. The federal census recorded 920,000 tractors on farms. For the first time, the USDA noted that farmers were acquiring neighboring farms to expand their holdings. Tractors allowed many farms to do away with hired help, improving family income. In 1940 the USDA counted slightly more than 1.5 million tractors across the United States, and that number

1955 Ford 850 V-8   This was not a Funk but certainly it was inspired by them and those that love them. Minnesota collector/restorer Doug Norman was not content with his tandem when the need for power struck him again several years ago. He installed a Ford Mustang 302 V-8 into the strong tractor chassis.

doubled by 1950. The trend toward farm enlargement was apparent and the tractor was largely responsible for that. By then, too, hired help was coming back on the farm.

"In 1953," Eddie Pinardi continued, "we had an NAA tractor that only held 10 gallons of gas. You send a man out and he could only work two hours before he had to come back and gas up. Now, with four plows, or five or six, we had to design the tractor to hold much more gas, as much as possible. We already had optional lights on those tractors so they could work later or go back out after supper.

"But once you got the operator out there, they're in the hot sun. Before, they were in every two hours, take a break, cool off, have something to drink before they went back out. When we got to doing the big tractors, we developed machines where you sent an operator out at six o'clock in the morning and he came back at eight o'clock at night on one fuel fill-up. You're the farm owner, you go fill him up instead of him coming in.

"I can't use a seat made out of steel like on the 8N. So I give them a padded seat, but it's not enough. You have one operator who weighs 150 pounds and another weighs 250, one 6 feet, 3 inches tall, the other 5 feet, 5. You make adjustments. Fit a shock absorber to soften the ride, add a spring.

"You put a cab on those tractors. Operator out there 12, 15 hours. Make it dustless, air-conditioned. Give them a radio. That's how everything developed."

At this point, Ford tractors had drifted some distance from Henry Ford's simple, lightweight machine to take the burden off the backs of man and animal. Tractors were market-driven. Ford's newly named Tractor and Implement Division was a survivor, one of nine full-line companies left after a tumultuous half-century of tractor making. Full-line manufacturers were those who produced not only tractors but a complete assortment of implements, wagons, accessories, and harvesting equipment under the same logo. In 1955 these nine were supplemented by 13 companies producing crawlers and 35 other firms manufacturing wheel-type tractors.

The leader was still International Harvester, enjoying the position it regained from Ford's 10-year-old Fordson in 1927 with its 3-year-old Farmall and its steady, solid gear-drive 10-20 and 15-30 models. Second was Deere & Co., followed by J.I. Case and then Massey-Harris-Ferguson. (This ranking was not computed in terms of tractor production but measured in gross revenues from all tractor, implement, and harvesting equipment sales.) Ford ranked ninth—last place. Product planners and marketing staff were scrambling. Expanding the product line seemed a sensible way to broaden the appeal of the red and gray tractors, to sell more of them and to climb in the ranking.

The other reason for the tractor line expansion had been even more purely internal business: In late 1954, Henry Ford II took FMC public. He offered shares of Ford on the New York Stock Exchange for the first time since 1919. This resulted from seven years hard work by Ernie Breech and Ford Division's

1955 Ford 850 V-8 It was Indianapolis 500-veterans Ab Jenkins and Barney Oldfield who demonstrated the value and performance of Firestone rubber tires on Allis-Chalmers' Model U tractors in 1931 and 1932. They would have killed for this kind of performance. With 160 horsepower available from its V-8 engine, this 850 would fishtail and spin its tires in every gear.

The Ford Model Lineup   The 1955–1958 production included the 660 utility, 741 Row Crop, 961 wide front, and 860 Standard. Each used either a 144-cid or 172-cid version of Ford's Red Tiger four-cylinder engine.

new president, Robert S. McNamara. McNamara arrived in 1948 with nine former U.S. Army Air Force statistical control systems managers. They had created accounting methods that could quantify everything from shells to soldiers. This group, directed by Charles "Tex" Thornton, a 32-year-old former colonel, was hired en masse. Stock and options in Dearborn Motors made it worth their while. From the start, they asked so many questions of other executives that they were dubbed Thornton's Quiz Kids. That name stuck until they began providing the answers themselves. They pulled Ford back from the

edge of bankruptcy and turned the company around financially. Their name changed to the Whiz Kids.

Prior to Edsel's death in 1943, Henry held 55 percent of the company stock, Edsel had 41.5, and Clara Ford controlled 3.5 percent. Before Henry's death in 1947, the family turned over nearly all the non-voting stock to the Ford Foundation, keeping control and decision making in family hands yet avoiding colossal inheritance taxes.

Eight years after his grandfather's death, Henry II was ready to let the public in, announcing that 10.2 million shares would be offered starting January 26,

1956. It opened at $64.50 per share. Within weeks, the offering sold out to 350,000 buyers, many of them farmers wanting to buy "some shares of Ford for the grandkids." The effect amounted to more than a massive infusion of cash. From 1919 until 1956, Henry and Edsel answered only to their own consciences for their decisions, good or bad. Now, 350,000 stockholders scrutinized and wondered. Before this, 10 Quiz Kids asked questions. Now Ford management had to satisfy thousands of inquisitors. This meant Ford's Tractor and Implement Division (FTID), like all other operations, had to pull its own weight. Competition was fierce, but not only from domestic makers. Ford's Dagenham works came within 5,000 tractors of matching U.S. production. If Dagenham offered a variety of tractors that American farmers wanted, domestic operations had better learn something. When Thornton's Quiz Kids asked what that lesson might be, Roeder and Brock's Tractor Engineering group responded with several new tractors offered in late fall 1954 as 1955 models.

Soon after FMC created its umbrella Ford Tractor Division, it expanded to encompass implements just after New Years 1954. Now, less than a year later, FTID Chief Engineer Dale Roeder and Assistant Chief Harold Brock unveiled FTID's response to a

1955 Ford 660 and 1958 741 Introduced in 1954, the 660 demonstrated Ford's new five-speed transmission and live PTO and hydraulics. It sold for $2,265 and developed 32.3 gross horsepower. The 741 with Ford's four-cylinder engine and its 900 twin were Ford's first tricycles. Both first appeared in the fall of 1955.

market demanding greater diversity. On January 6, 1955, FTID introduced its "New Era in Ford's Contribution to Agriculture," with its 600-series. This was derived from the NAA and eventually offered a full range of standard, row-crop, and utility configurations as well as three fuel choices. At the same time, they released the big brother 800-series. With the exception of a unit-frame prototype back in 1907, Ford had never produced a tricycle tractor. Six months after that introduction, Roeder and Brock supervised the opening of the Farm Machinery Research and Evaluation Center (FMREC), also in

Birmingham, in June 1955. This new facility offered a home for design, engineering, and test staff and its grounds included a test track and fields for tractor and implement development.

Ford's new 600 series used the NAA "Red Tiger" 134-cid inline four-cylinder engine. The model range began with the 640 with the Red Tiger still mated to the NAA's four-speed transmission. Higher trim models 650 and 660s used a new five-speed gearbox and the 660 included independent PTO (while 640 and 650 versions provided only dependent PTO.)

1957 Ford 961 and 1955 850   The top-of-the-line 961 offered live PTO and five-speed transmissions and used Ford's Red Tiger 172-cid engine, which also appeared in the 850 standard tread. The 850 models were not available with independent PTO, however (they came standard with dependent PTO), and they were offered only with Ford's four-speed gearboxes.

The 660s   Collector Doug Norman has begun gathering sets of tractors, including the product lineup shown elsewhere and these three 660 models. At right is the normally equipped 660 with power steering. In the center is a 660 ordered without power steering, and at left is the 1957 fully equipped 661 with live PTO.

The 800 series, also part of this "New Era" promotion, was more powerful, using a 172-cid engine derived from the Red Tiger but providing farmers with 40 horsepower. The 850 and 860 used the 650's five-speed transmission, and these were three-plow-rated tractors. The 860 also provided farmers with the 660's live PTO. Each of these six tractors was introduced only as a standard tread model. Row crops appeared in mid-April when FTID brought out its 740 (134 cid) and the 950s and 960s (using the 172-cid five speeds, and including, for the 960, live PTO). For decades, the company had offered only one model of tractor. Now it produced nine. That would last only until late-July when the 620

and 640 (134-cid) and 820 (172-cid) "Special Utility" models appeared. Only the 640 was offered with any hydraulics and each had only the NAA-derived four-speed transmission. They were meant primarily to pull lawn mowers and push snow plows for municipal and industrial customers. Initially, only gas engines were available, but in late January 1957, FTID introduced Liquefied Petroleum Gas (LPG) versions of both the 134- and 172-cid engines. The styling on each of these series still came from the NAA, and they retained Eddie Pinardi's shock of wheat within the restyled radiator grille badge.

For 1957 the Tractor and Implement Division performed cosmetic surgery on the entire lineup,

1956 Ford 660 Moto-Tug The transmission oil cooler of this Moto-Tug is visible at the bottom of the grille, and its fenders, cab, and rooftop amber rotating safety light are obvious. Used by the Minnesota Air National Guard and the U.S. Air Force as airplane tugs, these machines made full use of Ford's 22.4 drawbar horsepower.

adding a bold grid motif to the grille. These tractors, with a "1" added to their numbering systems, got names from Product Planning and Marketing staffs, eager to provide clear product identity. They called the small-engined models the Workmaster series, while they tagged the larger ones the Powermasters. Ford introduced LPG as a fuel option in mid-1957 across its entire range of tractors. The 19.2 gallon (working capacity) fuel tank replaced the gas tank; it and the other equipment necessary to operate on propane added about 100 pounds to the tractor weight.

Harold Brock's work was not always following the lead of product planners. The Division led the industry in its experiments in the late 1950s. Where

the 1930s and 1940s had been the "streamline age," the Fifties were the Jet Age.

In July 1957, Ford unveiled its "Typhoon," a free-piston diesel turbine engine installed in an extended 961 tractor chassis. Engineering built three. Its compound name masked the fact that it was two engines, not just one.

Ford's free-piston diesel engine used two pistons sliding to and from each other in a single cylinder. This engine needed only to produce exhaust gas, not reciprocal or rotary motion to move the machine. The pistons had no connecting rods. Ignition shoved them into "bounce cylinders" of compressed air at opposite ends of the combustion chamber. This

1956 Ford 850 Four Wheel Drive   This is one of the earliest versions of Elwood Engineering Company's four-wheel-drive conversions. At this time, the Wisconsin manufacturer adapted Dodge Power Wagon final drives and rear axles to the front drive. Later differential covers were stamped with the logo, ELENCO, unlike this early Dodge unit.

bounced them back toward each other, compressing new diesel fuel into ignition.

The exhaust gas ran a turbine driving double-reduction gears to which engineers Oscar Noren and Robert Erwin had connected main and auxiliary drives. The auxiliary operated the hydraulic pump and PTO while the main drive, reduced 5600:1 in first gear, moved the tractor. The turbine, running at 15- to 25-psi pressure, idled at 10,000 rpm and under load, reached 43,000 rpm. Capable of 100 horsepow-er, Noren and Erwin cautiously limited output to 50. They lengthened the 961 wheelbase 14 inches beyond the normal 85.3 inches to accommodate hardware necessary to create this system. At 4,200 pounds, it weighed 900 pounds more than a gasoline-engined 961. It stood 4 inches taller and 11 inches longer over-all. Noren and Erwin obtained fuel economy equal to that of other tractor engines. The benefit was that few-er moving parts cost less to replace and the entire engine experienced much less wear per hour.

1956 Ford 960 High Crop   Five speeds, four cylinders, live PTO and hydraulics, power steering, but gas or LPG only, the 960 Series was Ford's top of the line. By this time, Dearborn was producing Ford's high crops, offering 7 inches additional clearance by lengthening front spindles and enlarging rear wheel rims for the 40-inch tires.

1956 Ford 850 Four Wheel Drive
Elwood's kit included a single PTO shaft routed up to the front off-center differential (the better to straddle obstacles without high-centering the tractor). The box at right protects the operator's feet.

1957 Ford 501 Offset Diesel   Designed as a cultivating tractor to meet features that Deere, IHC, and Oliver had offered for some time, Dearborn's engineers moved the steering wheel and operator's seat about 8 inches off the centerline. These were very limited production tractors that were available only as high-clearance models.

Ford tractor dealer Harold Ypma of Ladysmith, Wisconsin, recalled the Typhoon passing through a neighboring village in far northern Wisconsin in late spring 1958.

"A truck and trailer from Ford Tractor Division stopped in for fuel and on it was a prototype, a turbine-powered tractor going to the Minnesota State Fair. When I went to the fair at Machinery Hill, they had a big roped-off circle and a guy was driving it around. You had to start it with compressed air. It had quite a sound."

The turbine howl was novel, but the engineers looked for practical applications. Free piston engines were fuel-inefficient but they and gas turbines had fewer moving parts than standard internal combustion gas or heat-ignition diesel engines. Repairs and rebuilds would be far less costly. Yet dust control was critically important and difficult to maintain in a farming environment. Ford's engineers concluded there was no practical application in agriculture for this compound, complex power source. But the complicated innovation that transmitted the Typhoon's turbine power to the ground was another story altogether. The shift-on-the-fly Select-O-Speed transmission, however, was one of Ford's sad stories that started at the end of the decade and lingered on into the 1960s before it was straightened out.

5

1958–1961

Dagenham's Power Major and Dexta Diesel Challenge Dearborn

Dagenham's reliable diesels went through steady upgrades and improvements between 1952 and 1956. John Fowler's engineers increased horsepower, although product marketing and sales personnel never promoted this fact. Diesel engines that had started at 34 horsepower at 1,400 rpm reached 37 horsepower at 1,600 rpm. In addition, in 1956, engineering switched from a single 12-volt battery on diesel models to two 6-volt batteries (the vaporizing oil and gasoline models stuck with the 12-volt single battery).

1958 Fordson Dexta   Dagenham's little companion tractor first appeared in 1958 using a three-cylinder version of the bigger E1A New Major's four-cylinder diesel. Designated the 957E during its nearly three-year development program, it became the Dexta, introduced to the agricultural press in London in late November 1957.

57

1958 Fordson Dexta   Full production of the Dexta began in February 1958, and in its first year, Dagenham turned out 22,444 models. Some 1,200 were shipped to the United States late that year. These ended up in the South, where both the need for smaller tractors and the appeal of diesel were greater. In the United Kingdom, Ford offered the Dexta in industrial and golf course models.

In early 1957, Dagenham introduced an industrial model (known more commonly throughout Britain as a "commercial" tractor) whose engine was designed to run at 1,800 rpm. (These applications, generally under much lighter load than four-plow-agricultural uses, allowed engineering to rate the engine at 44 horsepower and give users a top engine speed of 2,050 rpm for no-load transport purposes. The Industrial model also featured a single brake pedal operating dual rear brake drums mounted on half-axle shafts.) In April, F.M.C., Ltd., brought out the Mark II engine, the culmination of all the mechanical tinkering. With 51.8 horsepower at 1,600 rpm, it was something worth announcing, yet the sales and marketing staffs let it slip into the market-place almost invisibly. That was because the modified rocker arms, camshaft (engineering created one camshaft that it used in all its truck and tractor four-cylinder engines), cylinder head, enlarged-diameter fuel injectors, and deeper-stroke injection pumps presaged something more noteworthy to a conservative market-place: a Mark III version that would be known as the Power Major.

Even before the Power Major appeared as Ford's official entry in the horsepower contest, however, farmers needed something with a great deal more performance. County Cars and Roadless both had developed partial- or full-crawler conversions, and these made better use of the Major's power in regions where traction was a challenge. But even this was not enough for some farmers. And like many great improvements that had come earlier, this one came from farmers who wondered "what if?"

The answer came in 1957 from G. Prior, a farmer in Essex. Perhaps inspired by seeing wartime parachute-dropped scrapers devised by L. G. LeTourneau, Prior removed the front axles and wheels from two diesel Majors and hung the nose of the rear tractor from the hitch of the front one. He steered his invention from the rear Major where he could watch his plows, using a hydraulic system of his own creation. Others heard of his invention. Ernest Doe began to manufacture the tandem New Major, which he called the Doe Dual Drive or the "Triple D," at his workshops near Ulting, also in Essex. For farmers who needed 100 horsepower or more and were dedicated to Ford, the Doe tandem was the only option for another decade, until Ford Tractor Division— renamed in a reorganization in 1962—introduced its 105 horsepower Model 8000 in 1968. A year later, FTID brought out its first turbocharged model, the 9000, with 130 horsepower, and almost overnight tandem tractors disappeared from dealer catalogs and production lists. (Ironically, in 1964 Doe produced a tandem based on the Ford 5000,

1959 Fordson Dexta with Bush Hog   F.M.C., Ltd., produced the Dexta from 1957 through 1964. Stories abound concerning its unusual name. Some argue that it came from the nickname Texans give to a small steer, a "dexter." Others suggest more noble beginnings, from the Latin roots for the word "dexterous."

1959 Fordson Dexta Ford's engineers at Rainham Works fitted Perkins three-cylinder diesels in prototypes to produce the power output they desired for the Power Major's companion. Once Dextas reached production, Ford found it had insufficient plant space to manufacture engines itself. It did cast the blocks that Perkins assembled, however.

which gave his customers 130 horsepower. This would have been beneficial to those who already owned the models. With the advent of the turbo, however, farmers got the power of two tractors at the cost of only one.)

As author Allan Condie pointed out in his book, *Fordson New Major E1As 1951–1964,* the Mark II and Mark III—or Power Major—engines were easily recognizable from the intake manifold side. Intake ports on the earlier engines were staggered, while the redesigned cylinder heads placed the ports in a straight line. This engine would remain in use, substantially unchanged, through introduction and regular production (beginning in late October 1960) of the Super Major, until June 1962 when F.M.C., Ltd., announced the "New Performance" Super Major.

But, as Condie explained, while the engine persevered, the Power Major was possibly the shortest-lived production tractor in Dagenham's history (from 1958 through most of 1960).

The 1960 Super Major brought several new features to Britain's farmers, including a differential lock and an automatic pickup hitch coupled to the hydraulic power-lift system. Design engineers moved the headlights from alongside the radiator grille to within the stamped mesh grille because farmers were asking for a way to mount a front loader. Rear-mounted implements got a boost in efficiency as well; many of Harry Ferguson's three-point hitch and hydraulic depth-control patents (there were more than 150 in all) had expired and F.M.C., Ltd., already had applied much of the Ferguson technology to its

1960 Fordson Super Major   Ford produced the Power Major for just two years before introducing the Super Major to replace it. Its most significant improvement was its "Qualitrol" draft control and hydraulic system derived from the Dearborn tractors. In addition, Rainham engineers added a differential lock and disc brakes to start and stop more effectively.

new compact Dexta, introduced in 1958. On the Super Major, F.M.C. operated its top link (controlling lift and depth) as a compression link only, using gravity—and the drag of the plow or implement—to hold it down. The New Performance version, riding not on traditional Fordson red-orange wheels but now on new gray-painted wheels, became available in July 1963. It provided 53.7 horsepower and offered farmers a no-load engine speed of 1,925 rpm. These models included a drop control valve that effectively pushed the rear-mounted implements down, as well as more typically picking them up to maintain uniform soil penetration.

In advance of Dearborn's Whiz Kids and DMC's product planners, Dagenham's engineers began to recognize a market for a smaller companion tractor to its big Major line. As early as 1946, during one of Harold Brock's work visits, the engineering staff at Rainham Works took an 8 horsepower side-valve automobile engine from Ford's tiny Anglia automobile as well as its three-speed transmission. They mounted these mechanical elements and the radiator from the automobile on a stubby rail frame underneath crude tin-work. From all accounts the field trials went nowhere despite field experiments that

continued on page 66

The Yank in Sir Ernest's Court

"Mind if I call you Yank?" the older man asked. The yank, 39-year-old Ralph Christensen, didn't mind at all.

The speaker was Ernest C. Doe, an 82-year-old patrician businessman and manufacturer who, even in the early 1960s, wore a top hat to cover his balding head and carried an ebony walking stick. At that time, he was one of F.M.C., Ltd.'s largest customers.

Christensen was a farmer in central South Dakota. In April 1958, he had 780 acres to plow and plant and a full-time job that kept him off his land until evenings or weekends. So, "with a lot of work to do and no time," he fabricated a steel framework to mount two Fordson Majors nose-to-tail. He extended his subframe from the drawbar of the rear tractor forward to a 21-inch-diameter turntable. The subframe continued forward to attach to the engine and transmission of the forward machine. He placed the turntable below the engine on the rear tractor, mounted to

1961 Fordson Super Major Doe Dual Drive Ford introduced the Super Major in 1960. Rainham's engineers carried over the existing four-cylinder 3.94 x 4.52-inch diesel that appeared in the 1958 Power Major. Nebraska tests revealed that the diesel produced 42.6 drawbar horsepower and 47.7 horsepower off the PTO. One fast way to double that output was to double the tractor, to make a tandem.

pivot on its spindle, enabling the combination to turn tightly. It worked especially well after Christensen removed both front axles.

"It costs nothing to take them off," he said recently. "It takes horsepower to push those fronts. Whatever you've got on the ground better be working." Christensen steered his tandem hydraulically. He placed push-pull pistons on each side of the turntable. "I put them in the furrow," he said, referring to his tandem rig, "and I never changed a thing."

The two Fordsons gave him 100 horsepower, enough to plow, press, pack, and plant in one operation called "pony drilling." With his tandem attached to a seven-bottom John Deere plow and a 10-foot-wide drill, the entire system stretched 54 feet long. It got a lot of attention.

A story and pictures in the local paper alerted E. P. Johnson, the Ford distributor in Sioux Falls, South Dakota. Johnson came up with a group of observers who shot color slides and 8mm movies.

They sent these to Dearborn. Dearborn, however, had tricycles and Typhoons and was already experimenting with turbochargers. It had little interest in Dagenham's products, so it forwarded everything to Ford's design facility at Rainham. Engineers there contacted E. C. Doe, who already was building trenchers, planters, and other utility machines derived from English Fordsons or powered by their engines. At this same time, one of Doe's own customers in Essex, England, George Pryor, had developed a similar idea, though he had not fully sorted out the turntable configuration. E. P. Johnson's photos and films from South Dakota gave them the answers Doe needed. However, with no drawings available —Christensen even told Michigan State University he had no blueprints, only "drawings in his head"—Doe's staff got the big things right, but it missed some of the details. Those were the things that plagued Doe's customers for years.

Christensen had flown B-17s on 33 missions out of England during World War II. He understood the need for individual throttle controls for each engine. Doe tried to synchronize both Fordson engines with one throttle and a cable linkage

1961 Fordson Super Major Doe Dual Drive   There is some dispute over the origin of this idea, attaching one Fordson to another. Manufacturer Ernest Doe, producer of the Doe Dual Drive, or "Triple D" shown here, suggests a local English farmer approached him with a need for more power. South Dakotan Ralph Christensen knows he built one, removed the front wheels, and that Doe soon saw his in films.

between the two. Temperature and moisture variations made the Doe system imprecise and troublesome. From the start, Triple D users reported difficulty synchronizing engines.

Christensen built only one, his own, that he painted Owatonna green, the corporate colors of his full-time employer. By early 1961, Doe had his copies in production, and he was preparing a demonstrator model for the Smithfield Show in London in November. Meanwhile, another South Dakota man had approached Christensen to build a second for him. Christensen formed Tandem Tractors, Inc., with two friends, Jake Rabenberg, a John Deere and Oliver tractors and implements dealer in Selby, South Dakota, and Larry Manning, sales manager at Owatonna. About this time, too, Doe contacted Christ-ensen. His first question was, "How are we going to settle this thing?"

Doe was pleased and relieved to learn that Christensen was not a demanding man and that he had not patented his design. More than that, Christensen had enough work to do at Owatonna and his own farm. He didn't particularly care to become a manufacturer as well. He told Doe to produce tandems but instead of paying him a

1961 Fordson Super Major Doe Dual Drive   A large steel-plate frame supported the two tractors, hinged by a turntable beneath the front axle-point of the rear tractor. Hydraulic steering worked off the tractor's steering brakes and allowed the tandem to swivel nearly 90 degrees. Locking differentials gave extraordinary straight-ahead pulling power.

royalty, he asked Doe to designate Tandem Tractors as U.S. distributor. Doe invited Christensen to London, where they signed their agreement at a booth near the Doe Dual Drive on display.

"Tandem Tractor," Doe told him, "didn't sound distinctive enough," so he created the Triple D name. It could also be that it did sound too much like Christensen's company. Still the two men hit it off, the gentlemanly Doe taking Christensen into London for several dinners. "And don't call them tandems," Doe insisted. "Call them four-wheel-drive tractors."

Doe packed up three Triple Ds to ship to the port of Houston on a ship that also called at Brazil. He encouraged Christensen to exhibit the machines, and Christensen had already committed

to display one at the National Western Stock Show in Denver. When Christensen's crews arrived to pick up the tandems, U.S. Customs held up delivery. Customs inspectors found heroin stuffed into each intake and exhaust stack and only after they determined Tandem Tractors wasn't also importing drugs did they release the machines. The demonstrator barely arrived in time. Christensen's men weren't sure, either; they waited about three years before explaining the delay to their boss.

In all, Tandem Tractors imported just six Triple Ds to the United States. By then, Ford, Ltd., had introduced the Super Major, a new model plagued initially with engine and transmission problems. The amount of warranty work that these units

64

required troubled Christensen's bosses at Owatonna. They gave a choice: tandems or his day job. He stuck with Owatonna, a wise decision, as the arrival of Ford's turbocharged diesel tractors in 1963 gave farmers 100 horsepower without the complexity—or the $8,500 cost—of the Doe Dual Drives. (Doe itself determined the price, £1,950, about equal to three new Power Majors.)

Doe created 289 Power and Super Major Triple Ds through late 1964. Thereafter they based production on the English 5000 models. They called these Doe 130 and later, Doe 150 models. They manufactured another 170 of these more powerful, more sophisticated machines. But English regulations called for rollover protection safety cabs for operators. It was far too costly determining where and how to mount the roll-bars on each tractors. Doe discontinued production in late 1968. By that time Steiger, Wagner, and others had introduced powerful single-engined 4-wheel-drive models that eliminated all the lingering problems of the Doe Dual Drives.

Christensen's prototype was destroyed in a shed fire in 1971. His second subframe, fabricated prior to his agreement with Doe and still wearing its Owatonna green paint, now belongs to Doe Dual Drive owner Don Hagstrom in Colorado.

1961 Fordson Super Major Doe Dual Drive   Doe claimed more than 100 horsepower with the Triple D, a figure not available from other makers until turbochargers appeared in 1963. Co-inventor Ralph Christensen was U.S. distributor and brought in just six, each selling for about $8,500, or the cost of three Super Majors in the United States.

1960 Fordson Super Major Designers moved the headlights into the grille for farmers and operators who needed to use a front loader. Dagenham engineers also evaluated Dearborn's S-O-S transmission as well as other shift-on-the-fly systems including a hydrostatic transmission from Lucas. Dagenham manufactured 350 of these a day in 1960.

Continued from page 61

continued for another year or so. A second auto-tractor hybrid was born in 1950. This one, according to Stuart Gibbard, used a four-cylinder engine and transmission from the slightly larger Ford Consul automobile, mated to the rear axle of a production truck. Gibbard reported that Ollie Scholin, an American engineer who had been named F.M.C., Ltd.'s, chief engineer, supervised this project. Scholin had two prototypes assembled at Rainham, but these machines were prone to overheating. (Automobile engines are not meant for the constant-work loading that tractors normally perform. Cooling was so inadequate on this prototype that in trials, engineers boiled

the engine oil.) Gibbard went on to write that Scholin, like Brock before him, returned to Dearborn. Sir Patrick Hennessey named Mick Ronayne chief engineer. They killed the Consul prototypes and assigned John Foxwell to do his own designs.

One possibility that Gibbard points out is that Dagenham could simply have imported 8Ns. The terms of the Marshall Plan, however (to say nothing of Henry Ford II's own edict to do trade, not give aid), placed very high tariffs on goods imported to England and Europe from the United States. These import duties would have put Ford's 8Ns out of the reach of the farmers who needed them. In addition,

1958 Fordson Power Major on Leeford Rotaped Tracks Like Roadless and County Commercial Cars, Leeford manufactured kits to adapt Fordson tractors for marginal traction conditions. These six-plate tracks rotated around the large sprocket rear drive wheels using a complicated system of pulleys and chains. Power Majors replaced the one-year production 51.8 horsepower 1957 New Major.

Sir Patrick Hennessey believed strongly in the future of diesel engines and the affordability of the fuel. Dearborn had no diesels in its lineup and, worse, had no plans for them. It didn't need to; gasoline in the postwar United States was barely 12 cents a gallon.

But what if an 8N-sized tractor manufactured in the United Kingdom used an outside-built diesel? Ronayne and Sir Patrick decided in 1951 to adapt Dearborn's 8N for use with a Perkins three-cylinder diesel. Gibbard reported that several prototypes, involving more than 25,000 hand-built prototype parts and 2,000 drawings, resulted. The Dagenham engineering staff also worked with NAA prototypes and production models. Ronayne's staff adopted 8N and NAA front axles and steering and much of the hydraulic and draft control system, although to avoid the last of Ferguson's patents still in effect, Ronayne and his colleagues fitted a gear-driven hydraulic pump, powered by the PTO shaft.

John Foxwell, who had previously created a six-speed transmission from Dearborn's four-speed unit, replicated his work for this new prototype. Sir Patrick hoped to keep production costs to a minimum to keep the sale price down, so rather than acquiring diesels from Perkins, he asked Foxwell and Perkins to develop an engine Ford could manufacture

1958 Fordson Power Major on Leeford Rotaped Tracks   This photo gives no indication of the entertainment available while watching this machine in a field. Unlike traditional crawlers that use idler wheels to stretch the track and track rollers to support tracks on the ground, Leeford promoted this system claiming that it could easily be reconverted to wheel operation.

itself. They jointly created a 144-cid 32-horsepower three-cylinder diesel that Perkins referred to as the F3, based on its P3. It used a Simms fuel injection pump similar to the diesel Major. Sir Patrick also approved construction of a new foundry at Dagenham to produce the castings, engine blocks, and heads for the new NAA-derived diesel. With testing and development procedures similar to Dearborn's, the five complete mechanical prototypes of this new tractor, known internally as the 957E (for 1957 introduction, England), plowed more than 20,000 acres collectively through 1955 at Ford's Elvedon Estates. Sir Patrick and other officials and engineers introduced it in London in late November 1957,

christening it the Dexta. According to Gibbard, the tractor's original name had presented some unacceptable connotations in certain of F.M.C., Ltd.'s markets. So Sir Patrick and others selected the obscure "Dexta," perhaps as a play on the word "dexterous" ("having or showing skill in use of the hands, body, or mind") or "dexter," a heraldic term meaning "on the right-hand side" or "on the side of decency." Still another theory suggests it came from the Texan slang term for a small steer, a "dexter."

Regular production began in February 1958 with standard hydraulic draft control. It sold for £550, or about $2,640, with live PTO available as a £30 (roughly $144) option at the time. F.M.C., Ltd., manufactured 22,444 Dextas through 1958, including a shipment of 1,200 at year end to the southeast United States. In late May 1959, FTID inaugurated a vast sales and promotion effort. Within seven months, another 5,000 had reached U.S. shores to compete against Ford's own Workmaster and Powermaster lines.

In the United Kingdom, Dagenham offered a golf course model, and a Highway Dexta appeared with a foot accelerator, dual brake systems, front and rear fenders, rearview mirrors, and a tow hitch. Ford offered a 52-inch-wide vineyard model beginning in 1960, produced by Stormont Engineering in Kent. Then in November 1960, Dagenham introduced a slightly restyled version whose appearance more closely mimicked the new Super Major, including headlights set into the grille. In addition, as the last of the Ferguson draft control patents expired, Rainham's engineers relocated the hydraulic flow control valve to the pump side of the system. They created a limited availability gas engine for certain export markets and then in 1961, Dagenham offered a differential lock for the first time as standard equipment on the little tractor. A year later, in 1962, they followed up with the 960E, or Super Dexta, with the slightly larger 152-cid "Super 3" engine, developing 39.5 horsepower.

Through the early 1960s, Dagenham outproduced Birmingham, a fact not lost on management at World Headquarters (WHQ) in Dearborn. In 1960, Dagenham and Rainham turned out 71,500 tractors, an all-time record, according to Stuart Gibbard. In the next year, F.M.C., Ltd., reached two other milestones. It produced its millionth Fordson overall and its 500,000th Fordson diesel.

In March 1961, WHQ reorganized tractors and implements into Ford Tractor Operations, while it renamed Dagenham's Tractor Division into the Tractor Group, all under the umbrella of WHQ's Tractor Operations. Then in March 1962, WHQ took another step toward simplifying its operations into a single worldwide tractor program when it reorganized Tractor Operations into Ford Tractor Division (FTD). It designated the updated and renovated Highland Park factory in Michigan, its factory in Antwerp, Belgium, and a new plant at Basildon in Essex, England, as its exclusive production facilities for the new worldwide tractors.

Then four months later, U.S. operations unveiled its new color scheme, blue and gray, for all tractors worldwide, beginning with those machines manufactured at Highland Park. To fill out its product lineup, the new FTD imported Fordson Super Dexta and Super Major models, relabeling them the Model 2000 and 5000, successively, to slot into North American marketing plans. These also were painted blue and gray, while the same tractors remained dark blue and orange for U.K. sales until the 1964 model year, when FTD brought to the world its New Performance models. (The public introduction took place in early July 1963.) It was the beginning of the end of Fordson tractors and Dagenham production. A year later, with space at Dagenham desperately needed for English Ford automobile manufacture, and production at the Basildon plant on hold after WHQ postponed the Worldwide Tractor project introduction until year end 1964, FTD turned over Dagenham to passenger car engine manufacture. The Fordson tractor name disappeared. Henry Ford had created it in 1916 to shield himself. Anxious stockholders, greedy for their dividends from the profitable auto sales, wanted to tell him how to run his business. Now the name succumbed to profitable auto sales in England.

The tractors reappeared, manufactured in Barcelona, Spain. The government-owned Moter Iberia SA acquired the tooling and the production line and, according to Stuart Gibbard, it manufactured the Super Major as the Ebro 55 until well into the 1970s.

1957–1962

Workmasters, Powermasters, and Select-O-Speed Transmissions

For 1957, FTID performed cosmetic surgery on the entire U.S. production lineup. Dearborn's Whiz Kids had turned the company's financial fortunes around and FMC found itself in a position to add more staff, particularly at FTID and especially in product planning and marketing positions. Many of these new hires came from other mainline companies and their ideas had a familiar ring: Such-and-such company offers a so-and-so configured tractor (or implement). Why shouldn't we?

At FTID, this spawned a spurt of growth not seen in the tractor industry since the post-Depression mid-1930s when Massey-Harris introduced a general purpose four-wheel drive, Caterpillar brought out its diesel, and Oliver-Hart Parr startled the farmer's world with high-octane engines and smartly styled tractor tinwork. As the mid-1930s were for the rest of the tractor industry, the mid-1950s were for Ford's tractor engineers, stylists, marketing and sales staffs, and product planners.

1959 Ford 981 Select-O-Speed Demonstrator   This gas-engined demonstrator used the Powermaster 172-cid four-cylinder while the diesel carried over the 144-cid powerplant. The S-O-S also made it easier for operators to use PTO-driven implements over uneven terrain, shifting up or down to change ground speed while maintaining constant engine speed.

1959 Ford 871 Select-O-Speed Demonstrator

This was not an automatic transmission but a system of four planetary gearsets in series, shifted hydraulically. Engineers calculated gear ratios to apply engine power most efficiently. Top speed was 18 miles per hour at 2,200 rpm, but without changing engine speed, operators could gear down to 1.2 miles per hour in first gear.

The mid-1950s were a heady time in U.S. history. The Marshall Plan was working. European countries were trading with the United States, and there was a discernible air of prosperity and well-being in the air. While the Soviet Union, and to a lesser extent Communist China, were a threat to domestic tranquillity, Americans had children and bought cars and homes and President Dwight Eisenhower promoted it all with a vast network of Interstate Highways. These were ostensibly constructed as high-speed access routes for military troops to move from one coast to the other in the event of foreign invasion. But they became high-speed delivery routes for moving goods from the country to the swelling cities. The population growth—both in numbers of babies and dollars in circulation—and its shift from pre–World War II rural to post-War urban, meant farm equipment had to do more work to feed more mouths. To product planners, designers, engineers, and marketing people, this meant bigger, more powerful tractors with more features and greater capabilities than ever before.

Mechanized farming had changed as well. In 1910, American farmers planted 248.3 million acres. It took 135 hours of work to produced 100 bushels of corn and 106 hours to yield 100 bushels of wheat. By 1919 that land commitment in agriculture had increased to 279 million acres. At that time, nearly all farming was done with horses. Tractors on farms were used mostly for threshing. Horses and mules, which had numbered 21.5 million on farms at the turn of the century, sold for an average of $45 for a horse and $53 for a mule. By 1910 the population had increased to more than 24 million animals and their value had more than doubled. Horses brought $110, mules $130. Their number increased to 25.2 million in 1920, despite the world war's destruction, but horse prices had peaked in 1911 at $111 while mules continued upward to an average price of $147 in 1920. Yet in the war year of 1917 there were just

1959 Ford 871 Select-O-Speed Demonstrator
Ford produced the Select-O-Speed (S-0-S) demonstrators in Standard and Row Crop models, using gas or diesel engines. Collector and superb restorer Roger Elwood located an original gold-printed battery to finish his re-creation. The S-0-S allowed operators to effectively double drawbar power by downshifting two gears while moving.

1959 Ford 981 Select-O-Speed Demonstrator   Dealers and farmers alike remembered the gold tractors that Ford employed to introduce the new shift-on-the-fly transmission. Unfortunately, Ford rushed the transmissions into production to beat Deere, and these demonstrators and thousands of early S-O-S tractors spent more time in the shop than in fields.

15,525 farm tractors on farms in the United States. In 1919 manufacture surged to 314,953, of which half fell in the 20–22 horsepower range of the Fordson. Horse and mule populations slipped by 3 million in 1925 and by another 3 million in 1930, to 19.1 million. Horses could be had for $70 and mules for $84. These figures would plummet in the next three years as the Depression spread across the United States. Farm acreage had grown to 359.9 million acres in use in 1930.

In 1930, the USDA attributed a 30-percent increase in the value of crops per acre over a five-year period to better-designed, more-efficient, more-affordable tractors and implements. Henry Ford's all-black Model Ts had worked fine for their time. And his "any color so long as it's gray" Fordson and 9N and 2N tractors sold well enough. But as early as the 1930s, other manufacturers had learned that color appealed to the tractor buyer's family, and that appeal sold tractors. The lesson FTD had learned from painting its tractors in the colors of Harold Brock's wife's dress stayed with the company.

In 1956, tractors manufactured by F.M.C., Ltd., in the United Kingdom outsold the Michigan-built tractors for the first time. This would continue for nearly a decade and in some years, the plants at Rainham and Dagenham produced three times as many tractors as the U.S. plants at Birmingham and Highland Park.

Then in 1959, Ford Styling again revised the color schemes of each model, trying to recapture the market from its English cousins. Workmasters became red with gray trim, while the Powermasters added a red strip on the hood and now the Birmingham assembly plant painted the entire radiator grille red. In a further attempt to entice buyers, product planners created an offset tractor intended for farmers cultivating a single row or for those on smaller farms. FTID introduced the new model for the 1958 model year. This offset concept—Ford shifted the engine 8 inches to the operator's left—was similar to International Harvester's Farmall Model A "Cultivision" tractors, although the Ford 501 Workmaster Offset was a larger and slightly more powerful machine and farmers liked its Ford 144-cid diesel engine.

1959 Ford 621 Workmaster   This model was Dearborn Motors' basic workhorse. With neither PTO nor hydraulics, this tractor was delivered with only a drawbar. It was the natural successor to Henry Ford's stone-simple Fordson F. Many of these saw use pulling gang lawnmowers around golf courses and parks.

1959 Ford 841 Four Wheel Drive

A growing number of collectors, restorers, and enthusiasts are recognizing the interest and historical value of implements from this period. The visual appeal they add to antique tractors is immense. It educates viewers about the tools needed to work the earth, and it reminds others of the work they have done.

1959 Ford 971 High Crop Select-O-Speed The 971 was Ford's top model from 1957 through 1962, available either with Ford's 172-cid gas engine or the diesel. The Select-O-Speed provided operators with 10 speeds forward and two in reverse. Ford also offered LPG power, though only diesel or gas was available with the S-O-S.

Throughout the mid-1950s product planners gathered influence, and some say this was the beginning of Ford's decline in farm tractors. As it was with other companies at the time, competition between the manufacturers was very great. Each one wanted to be able to provide its customers with anything another maker offered. Often this led to a fair amount of "me-too-ism." The competition makes an offset cultivating tractor, for example. So must Ford. Sometimes, however, this led to a race to be first with a major innovation. Occasionally this urgent motiva-

tion led to product introductions before they were completely ready. Such was the case with Ford's most intriguing technological development, its Select-O-Speed transmission.

Harold Ypma, the Ford Tractor dealer from Ladysmith, Wisconsin, who saw Ford's experimental turbine-engined Typhoon in late spring 1958, remembered not only its sound.

"The one thing I did notice about it," he recalled, "was that it had a gearshift wand. It had the Select-O-Speed transmission.

"When I went to the fair, a guy was driving it around. It howled pretty good. But even more [dramatic] than the sound was the Select-O-Speed. They never said a thing about that, just the guy was changing gears while it was moving by sliding that wand up and down. Of course, that didn't come out until the next year. I was watching them shift the gears on the go."

In the reports that Ford published in the Society of Automotive Engineers' journals in July 1957, the transmission was briefly listed in a specifications box as a "full power shift, 10 speeds forward-2 reverse."

1961 Ford 671 Select-O-Speed with Ford Disk   Manufactured from 1957 through 1961, the 671s were offered as diesel or gas-engined tractors with either 32 or 34 gross horsepower, respectively, but only with the Select-O-Speed transmission after 1959. The 3,028-pound tractor sold new for $3,105, not including the Ford Model 101 combination disk harrow.

1961 Ford 741 Workmaster   Ford made both its 700 and 900 series tractors available as row-crop narrow front models and standard configurations. This gas-engine version used Ford's simple four-speed transmission but it was equipped with power steering and the remote hydraulic valve to operate front-mounted or under-mounted implements.

For FTID, the introduction of the Select-O-Speed was as exciting as bringing into the world the Ford-Ferguson 9N with its three-point hitch and hydraulic system had been. And, almost as quickly, it proved just as frustrating to its engineers as taming Ferguson's hydraulics had been 20 years earlier.

The first tractor assembled with the Select-O-Speed, serial number 60949, was manufactured on January 16, 1959. It was part of a fleet of Model 861

introduction tractors painted gold and provided to Ford's distributors. The Select-O-Speed was not an automatic transmission. It was a collection of four planetary gear sets in series, one behind the other. This configuration gave the operator full control of gears, engaged hydraulically, whenever desired. There was no longer a clutch. An "inching" control allowed forward or backward movement with critical accuracy. The operator shifted the tractor while moving and Ford

1959 Ford 971 High Crop Select-O-Speed LPG   Ford introduced LPG, or propane, as a tractor fuel for the 1957 model year. Propane cost less than gas or diesel, burned cleaner, and because of the higher compression required to use the fuel, was more efficient in output and fuel economy than gasoline.

engineers conceived the gear ratios to apply the engine's power most efficiently. For example, down-shifting from sixth to fourth gear doubled the draw-bar pulling power while coming down from 10th to fourth increased pull by eight times.

One clear benefit was for PTO use over uneven terrain. The operator could shift down or up while maintaining steady engine speed. This meant there was less risk of any PTO-driven implement jamming. Top road speed was 18 miles per hour at 2,200 rpm in 10th gear, yet without varying engine speed, the operator could gear down continuously to as slow as 1.2 miles per hour in first gear.

"Engineering the tractor is different from an automobile," FTID's chief engineer Harold Brock said, "because the tractor is under more sustained load. On the transmission for an automobile, you can test it in low gear under full power and if it lasts 45 minutes, it's a good transmission. In a tractor you put it in low gear and you have to run it thousands of hours. Because that's the way it's going to be working. So the durability and the testing of tractors is more severe than cars. And of course, you're off the road, running into ditches.

"There's a lot more of real engineering that goes into the tractor. Today we have computers and finite analysis. We can do a lot of design and experimentation in the computers before we ever build a prototype. Whereas with the little tractor, the 9N, most of the people working on it were not even engineering graduates. The master mechanics back then, what we'd call technicians today, they were the engineering people doing the design work of those days.

"We designed somewhat by proportion and somewhat by experience. We did a lot of testing," Brock continued. "We didn't have the sophisticated testing procedures and equipment we have today. So instead we just overdesigned things a great deal. We didn't know. So we always added more metal than we needed. Today you can nearly calculate how much metal you are going to need. And because of the expertise, engineers sometimes make things too light. They get too close to the edge and they get in trouble."

The Select-O-Speed got in trouble. Early production models would not run very long before they'd fail. It was attributed to several causes, but in the end the Tractor and Implement Division warranted a great number of tractors. A product planner with great influence at Ford's WHQ in Dearborn had

1971 Ford 971 High Crop Select-O-Speed LPG
The LPG tank, regulator, and vaporizer added about 100 pounds to the overall heft of this 5,970-pound machine. The tank was labeled a 24-gallon capacity but expansion allowance took about 20 percent, with an actual fuel capacity of roughly 19.3 gallons.

learned that Deere was working on a powershift transmission. He really wanted Ford to come out with it first, no matter what.

"It wasn't ready," Eddie Pinardi recalled, "it just wasn't ready. We'd say, 'Well, maybe it's this end. We'd fix that end to what we thought it should be and then something else popped up over there. It wasn't one of those products where you could look at something,

1961 Ford 6000   With Select-O-Speed transmissions, full hydraulics, and PTO, the first 6000s weighed nearly 6,900 pounds. These tractors reflected the space-age styling sweeping auto, truck, and industrial design worldwide. They were meant to compete with Deere's new 4010, the 840-series from Case, the Oliver 1800s, and IHC's big 660s.

figure out what the problem was, fix it, and forever after it's a fine product. This was one case where we could not find the problem.

"We brought in different engineers. They'd last a while and they'd go back. The next set would come in and finally nobody wanted the job. Solve one problem and something else would go. Why? Because a hole is too small for the oil to go through. So we'd fix that but then something else would fail. It wasn't just as simple as gears overheating and failing. We finally redesigned the whole thing, based on everything we learned from all the fixes that didn't quite do the job.

They just redesigned the whole thing. And then it went on to be a fine product."

One other project kept Ford engineers challenged, but much more pleasantly, through the mid- to late 1950s. This, as with the Typhoon, was a tractor not meant for production but simply to test the limits of imagination and technology at the time. C. B. Richey took an 841 Powermaster standard configuration model and created an autopilot tractor. It became nicknamed "The Sniffer," because it was guided by a small wire imbedded in a concrete test track at Ford's Engineering Research Center in

1961 Ford 771 Powermaster Select-O-Speed Diesel By the 1960s, Ford's product planners for both automobile and tractor divisions, intending to compete with Chrysler and GM, Deere, Case, IHC, and others, offered combinations and options to appeal to all buyers. This shift-on-the-fly row crop used Ford's diesel for power, requiring taller exhaust and air-intake stacks.

1961 Ford 6000
In its Nebraska tests, the 6000 gas six-cylinder developed 63.1 PTO horsepower at 2,227 rpm. The 223-cid engine used nearly square bore and stroke, at 3.62 x 3.6 inches. It achieved a maximum drawbar pull of 59.3 horsepower in sixth gear, tugging 4,473 pounds behind the tractor, which had been ballasted up to 9,535 pounds total.

1962 Ford 871 Select-O-Speed Four Wheel Drive   By the time Elwood Engineering Company had reached the early 1960s, it had revised its front drive system to such an extent that it embossed its name on the differential cover. Remarkably, the rest of their system was pretty much unchanged over a decade or so of manufacture.

Birmingham, Michigan. One small antenna set between the front wheels picked up a signal that provided directional information, and a second antenna received a signal instructing the driverless tractor to operate brakes, clutch, or implement lift. Practical applications for this system were limited by the

necessity at the time to submerge the wire in a field. No one solved the risk of rows that would be harvested and tilled again for the next planting. Still, Richey's tractor system proved of great benefit for engine and transmission durability tests, evaluations that could be performed on a hard surface. By the

1961 Ford 6000 If Ford thought it had seen trouble with its Select-O-Speed transmissions, that was just a warm-up for the initial 6000 production. Components and systems failed, leaving farmers stranded in the fields. Ford generously replaced entire tractors under warranty.

1961 Ford 871 Select-O-Speed Four Wheel Drive
With the second generation S-O-S transmissions, the 871 was a pretty pleasant package to operate. With its four-cylinder 3.90 x 3.60-inch diesel providing plenty of low-end torque, there was little this package couldn't accomplish around the farm, despite having just 41 PTO horsepower.

time journalists and invited guests saw it in late May 1958, it had been in use testing tractors at Birmingham for three years.

Throughout the early 1960s, Ford in England (and in Michigan) experimented with a variety of drivetrains including torque converters and a hydrostatic transmission. Rainham Works got a revised and improved Select-O-Speed in mid-1961 and by late summer, it had a running Super Major with the

10-speed transmission installed. But this was duplication of efforts, both in experiments and in offering separate tractor models for different markets. It had proven unwieldy and inefficient from both cost accounting and production perspectives. Like a morning sun, the need for change was on the horizon and it was rising steadily.

Epilogue

From 1960 onward, the unstoppable march toward "World Tractor" began. In the United States, FTID had begun paying attention to the municipal, industrial, and construction markets for the 1959 model year, introducing tractors with front loaders, rear-mounted backhoes, and other earthmoving equipment. Product planners had exhausted the hundreds-numerology and, to simplify designations, they renamed the Workmaster industrial series as 2000s while Powermasters became 4000-series models. In August 1960, FTID introduced its heavy duty 4,000-pound capacity 4000-series forklift. At the end of the year, industrial and construction models got a new paint

1963 Ford 6000 Sporting the new Ford World Tractor color scheme, replacing Dearborn red with Dagenham blue, the 6000 was otherwise unchanged. As part of the World concept, Ford offered gasoline, diesel, and LPG fuel options. The 6,895-pound tractor developed nearly 61 PTO horsepower in tests at Nebraska.

1963 Fordson Super Major Dagenham's tractor operations faced extinction as these 1963s appeared. Ford, Ltd.'s, need to produce more automobiles laid a stronger claim to manufacturing space while the Highland Park facility near Dearborn was underutilized. A new plant at Basildon, England, took over and Super Majors became the Ford 5000 in 1965.

scheme, retaining Ford red but exchanging the gray-beige for yellow.

For agricultural tractors, Ford World Headquarters made an effort at peaceful reconciliation between competing design and manufacture teams. FTID proposed a politically correct color scheme that retained the two-tone combination of U.S. tractors. The new color choices carried over the domestic gray used in its ag models. However, the Ford red was replaced with Fordson blue. Corresponding with industrial and construction models, FTID renumbered ag models using the 2000 (on the machine derived from Dagenham's Super Dexta) and 4000 ranges. Then in 1961, Ford Tractor Operations (FTO) replaced FTID

Missouri farmer Royal Hoyer puts his nearly 28-year-old Fordson through its paces, its rakes spinning, over a section of hay in southwest Missouri. Plotters and planners in Dagenham and Dearborn were already at work converting Super Majors to World Tractor Model 5000s for 1965, when the name Fordson disappeared.

1963 Ford 2000   In March 1961, Ford underwent the first of several international tractor operation consolidations, bringing together Dearborn's Tractor and Implement Division and Dagenham's operations. It announced formation of a worldwide tractor line and soon introduced the Model 2000, replacing Dearborn's 601 series machines.

1964 Ford 2000 LCG   The LCG abbreviation stood for Low Center of Gravity. This industrial model, derived from the late 1950s industrial configuration 601s, was ordered and optioned for golfcourse work in Illinois.

1964 Ford 2000 LCG Carrying over the 661's 172-cid engine and its standard power steering, the gas-burning model also had live hydraulics, its pump sitting behind the coil and below the battery. Its wide stance and rear dual wheels gave it exceptional stability on hilly terrain.

as the umbrella group for both U.S. and U.K. planning and production. Its first product was the Model 6000 with new six-cylinder 223-cid gas or LPG engines and a new 242-cid diesel. FTO sourced all three engines from Ford medium-duty F-500 and F-600 U.S. trucks and revised them to manage tractor operating characteristics.

Nomenclature changed yet again in 1962 when Tractor Operations became FTD. This nudged the worldwide corporation another step toward its world tractor concept. At this point, England's Fordson Super Major became the new

Ford Model 5000. Yet confusing introductions still occurred. In mid-1962, FTD brought out its low center-of-gravity tractors, the LCG models. Designated 1963 models, they still retained the sheet-metal styling derived from the 1953 Golden Jubilee. The LCGs also were painted in the interim 1960 industrial yellow and red coloring. FTD conceived and marketed them for highway road mower and golf course uses where side hills might topple taller, narrower tractors.

By 1964, Dagenham had ceased producing Fordson tractors and FTD had simplified its line, returning

1964 Fordson County Super Six

County Commercial Cars produced its first six-wheel Ford trucks in 1929. It began producing crawlers based on Fordsons in 1948 and its "Fourdrive" 4WD products grew from its crawlers, creating first a Super Four and later, using a Ford six-cylinder industrial engine, the County Super Six.

1964 Fordson County Super Six   The 590E industrial diesel produced about 70 gross horsepower at 2,200 rpm. Each front wheel, whether for its crawlers or the Fourdrive 4WDs, was powered by its driveshaft outside the frame. These shafts came off County's own rear-axle housing assembly providing forward PTO outputs.

to standard configuration models (except for a tricycle Model 6000). Ford discontinued offset tractors and the rest of the ricycles as issues of tractor safety and stability, roll-over protection, and owner and operator liability began to appear in dealerships, boardrooms, and courtrooms. By the end of 1964, the new U.K. facility in Basildon was up and running and FTD's three tractor plants (Basildon, its new operation in Antwerp, Belgium, and Highland Park, Michigan) began producing the 2000, 3000, 4000, and 5000 series, part of the latest 6X design configuration that unified, at last, Ford's tractor image worldwide.

The 1960s were an interesting period of time in the United States and throughout the world. As FMC makes more of its archival information available and as collector interest grows in the machines manufactured during this period, there will surely be a more in depth look at Ford Farm Tractors of the 1960s.

Index